Can Christians Be Educated?

Can Christians Be Educated?

A Proposal for Effective Communication of our Christian Religion

MORTON KELSEY

Compiled and Edited
by Harold William Burgess

RELIGIOUS EDUCATION PRESS INC.

Mishawaka, Indiana

Printed in the United States of America

Library of Congress Cataloging in Publication Data

Kelsey, Morton, 1917–
  Can Christians be educated?

  1. Christian education. I. Title.
BV1471.2.K44   207   77-3691
ISBN 0-89135-008-X

3 4 5 6 7 8 9 10

Religious Education Press Inc.
Box 364
Mishawaka, Indiana 46544

*Religious Education Press Inc. publishes books and educational materials
exclusively in religious education and in areas closely related to religious
education. It is committed to enhancing and professionalizing religious education through the publication of significant scholarly and popular materials.*

Contents

Foreword

Religious education has been one of the most important and visible endeavors of the church since the earliest years of the Christian era. But over the centuries this effort has changed. Originally Christian education was a necessity. When the church itself was young, it had to be certain that new Christians understood the experiences that had come to them well enough to communicate such experiences to others without betraying the whole community into the wrong hands.

Later, as the church came to feel secure, the need to work with adults seemed less acute. Gradually the emphasis shifted to an attempt to teach young Christians to become loyal and useful members of the Christian community. Much of the time this effort has been successful because the church understood—or sometimes simply sensed—what kind of experiences were needed and whether its major appeal should be made to the head or to the heart.

Today however, as at several points in the church's history, it has become apparent that our religious education is not effective enough, and that some kind of improvement is needed. The suggestions for change seem to come in all sizes and shapes. Some thinkers look to theology to provide an approach, while others are convinced that most of our reflection and research about the problem must relate to the teaching-learning process. Sadly enough, many changes in the church's educational practices have been proposed and adopted without the reflection and research necessary to find out what will work. As Charles Melchert has so accurately observed, a decision to make some change in the way religion is taught may mean little more than that someone has decided to "do it differently."

In some of our Christian churches the problem of developing a really effective program of religious education has become so acute that the question has been seriously raised, "Can Christians be educated?" For more than three decades Morton Kelsey has tried to find answers to various statements of this question. He has worked with vestries and with the religious education council of his church, in the counseling room, in conferences and workshops across America and in other countries, as well as in the quiet of his own study, trying to find the best answers. In recent years he has worked with this question in the classrooms of the University of Notre Dame. His reply to the question is a resounding YES. "Christians," Morton Kelsey says, "can be educated." This book is a statement of what he has found are the most effective ways of communicating the reality of Christianity to people both young and old.

Professor Kelsey is consistent in rejecting the either/or formulations which have so often constricted our thinking about Christian education. For example, it is clear that he considers religious education a matter of the heart as well as of the head. Or again, his approach to religious education keeps him from fitting neatly either into the ranks of those who view its theory and practice primarily as theological problems, or into the ranks of those who try to state all of the problems simply in terms of some particular theory of education. On the contrary, he suggests that our first job is to consider the various reasons for trying one idea or another in order to see whether or not we are promoting the kind of religion we want people to follow.

This book, then, does not offer a set of cookbook answers to worn-out questions. Rather it proposes a way of thinking about the process of religious education, based on some very practical suggestions for going about the practice of it. To describe this way of thinking, Kelsey draws in turn upon biblical, theological, philosophical, psychological, and educational insights. He makes a good deal of sense. He helps one to think and to take action.

Personally, I wish to thank Professor Kelsey for the opportunity to work with him on this book, mainly in selecting and organizing the materials, and in editing them somewhat. The sequence of ideas, it should be noted, follows a nontraditional pattern of placing the more practical issues early in the book, leaving the more theoretical matters for the later chapters. The first chapter, for instance, is a testimony to the fruitfulness of these practices, which were developed and adopted in the Monrovia, California, parish of which Fr. Kelsey was rector during the 1950s and 1960s. The final chapter, on the other hand, is a brief, readable statement of the theoretical rationale for his approach to religious education—and, in fact, his approach to the entire Christian ministry.

The references and a selected bibliography are given at the conclusion of the text so that the reader who is interested in pursuing the ideas Professor Kelsey presents may do so.

In addition, I wish to thank Mrs. Paisley Roach for her help in editing the text of this book, and also Mr. Rodney Moyer for the insights and the encouragement he offered me.

HAROLD WILLIAM BURGESS

Preface

The Christian church has taken a terrific battering in recent years. Some competent thinkers have even suggested that the loss of dedicated members of the church may continue and even grow worse. There is a real question in many minds as to whether the Christian church can continue to propagate itself, can continue to pass on the faith and practice of Christianity. Can modern Christians really be educated? Can the traditional faith be passed on to modern men and women?

For nearly thirty years I have been engaged in the practice of demonstrating that the Christian message can indeed be passed on to modern people and that nothing else can meet the need of the modern person as much as essential Christianity. For twenty of these years I was engaged primarily in a parish, on the firing line. For the last eight years I have been teaching in the department of graduate studies in education at the University of Notre Dame. My task there was to show teachers of religion methods by which they could facilitate a relevant appreciation of Christianity among adults and children in the twentieth century.

The articles from which this book was drawn were attempts to deal with various aspects of the problem of communicating Christianity. The problem is approached from a practical point of view and from the point of view of theology. We then look at the teaching of prayer, Christian love, emotional development and human wholeness. If we are to deal with any of these subjects we must have a consistent point of view and a theory from which to operate. We cannot communicate to human beings unless we have an understanding of who they are and how they function. We must also use the well-established discoveries of research in education. Few religious educators know these data and have an adequate theory of personality.

I am deeply grateful to Harold William Burgess, a most competent religious educator in his own right, for gathering these papers together and for his work in planning, compiling, and editing. It was he who first suggested that there was a need for a book of these reflections on Christian education. I am also deeply indebted to Paisley Roach who worked with me on the original articles and also on their final form in this present book.

1

A Parish Model for Educating Christians

Several years ago I was asked to speak to a diocesan conference of educational leaders in the Catholic church. I had an afternoon and an evening with the group before it was my turn to address them, and as I listened I began to sense a mood of tension and gloom. The speakers were presenting excellent ideas; they were making good practical suggestions, but something was missing. They were met by a feeling of frustration and confusion. I started my remarks by mentioning the chaotic, hopeless feeling that overtakes any educator who is trying to bring Christianity to others.

The statement of this fact—which seemed about as commonplace as the nose on one's face—brought down the house. An outburst of laughter released the tension, and the barriers were broken down. For this group of Catholic educators the problems seemed insurmountable. They seemed to face a morass which absorbed their efforts, leaving hardly a trace. Before the problem could be attacked, or even considered, the seriousness of the crisis in Christian education had to be faced.

The same despair faces religious educators in nearly every segment of the church. For a number of years I have been teaching in the graduate department of education at the University of Notre Dame in close contact with the nuns and priests and layworkers who are trying to bolster the sagging educational venture in the Catholic church. I have also had students who are professionals coming from almost every major Protestant group. I myself had been through the heroic attempt of the Episcopal church to introduce the "Seabury Series" and the ideas of group dynamics into its religious education. I had done my best to work with the "Group Life Labs," and then watched the program fall flat on its face with more than a million dollars down the drain. But the final blow to my WASP heritage was exposure to the problems of the Catholic church which had always seemed immune to defeat. At last I was forced to admit that the business of communicating Christianity to contemporary man is in dire trouble.

I have found only one major exception. Where a religious group has been able to hide from contemporary society and separate itself from the world, from modern science and philosophy and drama, then children and adults may still be indoctrinated. There are a number of groups attempting to do just this which keep growing in size. In uncertain times defensive measures often seem better than none at all; yet there are real problems with an approach like this. One cannot force people to put on blinders simply because they need Christianity. In fact, I wonder if such groups can really reach out to the needs of the modern world and touch people where they are today with the essential Christian message.

An Experiment Which Worked

Is there any alternative to this way of dealing with Christian education? I believe there is. For nearly ten years, in the parish of which I was rector, I saw a very different program of Christian education at work. It started with a remarkable woman, Dr. Ollie Backus, who is a professional educator in the field of speech therapy. She had received a Ph.D. in both speech therapy and neuroanatomy in the early thirties. When the psychological factors in speech correction were beginning to be recognized, she investigated group dynamics early in its development at Bethel, Maine. She had already realized that the mechanics of correction gave the child with speech problems and his parents only a partial answer. The problems of both could be helped far more effectively when there was concern for the individual and recognition of his need to tap resources beyond himself and the group. Dr. Backus realized that this is essentially a religious need, and she began to read C. G. Jung.

She and her colleagues discovered how deeply Jung's understanding spoke to them.

When I first met Ollie Backus she was teaching at the University of Southern California. She had come to California to further her study of Jung and had heard of our attempt to integrate some of his ideas into our church life. She came to church to find out. After the service we talked. I mentioned the clinic, the two or three classes, the preaching and prayer groups which gave a Jungian orientation to our program. She spoke of finding the need to use religious principles in her own work. Then she made the incredible suggestion that perhaps *we could do a better job of Christian education if we used religious principles in teaching Christianity.* She explained that our educational method, as well as the content, could reflect and help to transmit the basic Christian ideas about the depth of human beings and their relations to other people and to God.

This sounded exciting to me, and since the church had just lost its director of religious education, we decided to try working together to put this idea into effect in the parish. The one unconditional requirement was to admit that educating Christians is important and to take it as seriously as preaching or financing church buildings or conducting rummage sales. This was a radical proposition, but I stuck my neck out and proposed to the vestry that we try it.

First of all, it would cost money. There was no reason for the church to expect Dr. Backus to work for us for less money than she had already been offered to teach at the state university. Nonetheless, the idea of Christian education being important enough to require the church to pay for it was shocking to the group of business men on the vestry. In my twenty years in the parish nothing was more traumatic for them than the idea of supporting such a program—not even starting a psychological clinic, or the development of charismatic groups, or the time when there was an outburst of tongue speaking during the church service. It continued to be a problem. There was even a time when I had to suggest resigning, telling the vestry that if Ollie Backus went, I went also.

The greatest difficulty arose from the fact that money had to be laid out to train teachers long before we could look for any results with children, probably for as long as five years. A teacher can only communicate as much Christianity as he or she has assimilated and *is living*. It was not easy for any of us to realize how little the average member of the church understood about the reality of Christianity, and how much less they lived it. Dr. Backus began to see that most teacher recruits were exhibiting both a lack of knowledge and an even more inadequate example of Christian life. She found our average church family no more mature or Christian-oriented than the average parents of children with psychological speech problems. This was a stunning jolt to both of us.

The Method

Obviously the first task was to work with adults so that there would be teachers who could work with children without deepening the rut of ignorance and failure. Dr. Backus proposed an adult education program of which any graduate school of education would be proud. Except for the introductory class—which offered an understanding of the nature of this world in which we live and which was required of everyone—the classes were limited in size to fifteen. Every member paid a small fee, and they were expected to attend every class *on time*. If anyone was continually late or absent without a good reason and without having informed the instructor ahead of time if possible, the person was dropped from the class. Learning about our religion was considered just as important as any college class for credit.

I was certainly skeptical about whether people would tolerate such conditions in a church program, and there were some tense moments. But as the word spread that real learning about Christianity and life was taking place, people began to come from all over the area. The number of classes had to be increased, and before long there were waiting lists for most of them. Members of the church who lived nearby and some people from more than fifty miles away came faithfully. During the first ten years the lives of over three hundred adults were touched by this program.

The classes were nearly all seminars, making it possible to join real knowledge with genuine education through method. Executives of nationally known businesses came to take part when they found people were learning about Christ and life and themselves in a depth to which they had never before been exposed. Men and women, high school drop-outs, doctors and lawyers rubbed shoulders with each other. Each found that they had something to communicate to the other. *This was Christianity in action.*

It is strange how the educational world, particularly at the college level, still clings to outdated methods of teaching, seemingly unaware of the evidence that has piled up against them. The lecture method of teaching has been shown to be the least effective way of conveying either facts or values to the student. A veritable mountain of evidence has been amassed, as James Michael Lee has shown so clearly in his books on religious education, *The Shape of Religious Instruction* and *The Flow of Religious Instruction.* For the individual who can read for himself, the lecture method is a bore—except in those rare instances where the teacher is either a dramatist or a clown. In the seminar method, the students read the material before coming to the group. They then bring their questions and doubts, as well as any special information, into the group interaction. Here teachers are able to bring their knowledge and experience directly to bear upon the needs of students as individual problems are revealed. Thus they are able to deal with individual needs in a way that is usually not possible.

The seminar method of teaching is based on a very different view of human beings than most other methods. Until recently, most educational theory has considered the individual just a blank slate on which the skillful teacher can write by using such tools as operant conditioning. Yet men and women are bigger than we have thought, and the seminar method tries to take this into account. As depth psychology suggests, each individual has a rich and complex unconscious as well as what is seen in our conscious minds. Each of us brings to the education group our own basic type stucture, our own history and understanding of words and ideas. Only as each of us is treated as a distinct and unique person can education begin to reach us at a level of our own need. Then we really listen to what is said and try to integrate its significance into our lives because we want to. If this is true of teaching mathematics and the social sciences, it makes even more sense in Christian education which is concerned with a way of life perhaps more than with a set of ideas.

Trying to communicate religion today without some knowledge of depth psychology and educational methods is just as foolish as it would be for a missionary to go to some underdeveloped, poverty-stricken country without a knowledge of medicine, hygiene and agriculture. If Christians want to share their religion with others, they must know the nature of the persons they are teaching, their uniqueness, their hang-ups, their backgrounds, and how they can be taught. This is at the heart of Jesus' stress on the individual and on loving the individual. *It is impossible either to love or to educate anyone whom one has not taken the trouble to know and understand.* Love for the starving person involves realizing his hunger and need, for the sick understanding his illness, for the uneducated in Christ finding out what that individual is like and how he or she can be reached.

The Content

It is very difficult for human beings to realize that several kinds of effort and several kinds of material may be required for a course of action. Method is certainly important if the educational endeavor is to succeed, but specific content is just as important for Christian education. Both are necessary. Teaching religion requires real effort, skill, and knowledge if it is to be effective with the questioning, liberated men and women of today, young or old. One of the problems of modern men is that they have questioned to the point of eliminating religious content. Liberation has meant being brainwashed into believing that there is no level in the universe which provides us with specific religious knowledge. Most theologians and religious educators have gone along with this assumption, not questioning it in spite of the fact that almost every such total assumption is at least partially untrue.

If we are to work with either the method of Jesus of Nazareth or the content of his teaching, and that of the early church about him, one of the first tasks we face is to rethink the way modern thought approaches the world. The present idea that man is limited to a one-level universe is foreign to the outlook of Jesus, and also to believing that Jesus was the one the early church said he was. These basic teachings both tell us that human beings are in touch with a spiritual world as well as a physical one. The reality of the Risen Christ and the likelihood of life beyond death both occur in the spiritual world. It is from that world that the Risen Christ can still touch modern men and women, changing their lives and environment as well as having a moral effect which can help them to make those changes on their own initiative.

Changing people's basic outlook, however, is difficult; it is usually much easier to change their morals. With this in mind, the classes in our program of religious education were graduated. The first class, in which a basic world view was presented, was required of everyone and had to be completed before registering for any other course. Ministers, staff, and everyone took this basic material, in which it was suggested that none of us knows enough to assume that we human beings are confined only to sensory experience and a physical world. The individual's spiritual experiences, his prayer life, his religious intuitions should be examined and sifted and used as carefully as one's sensory experiences.

We could find plenty of theological material denying that people might still be touched by God. Bishop Robinson, Rudolf Bultmann, and various others have not been backward about discussing their ideas. But since we could find little which suggested that individuals can become open to genuine religious experiences, Dr. Backus prepared mimeographed material to introduce students to this idea. Picking and choosing among the best of modern thought, she showed how often scientists and sometime even philosophers—often without meaning to—open the door to taking the experiences of religion seriously. Some of the more important psychological material supporting this view was presented.

People began to see that the New Testament, and the Old as well, could be taken quite seriously. The actions of power, the visions and dreams and healings, the discernment of spirits, supernatural wisdom, prophecy, and tongues came to have more and more meaning for the students. These experiences could be taken as seriously as the moral admonitions of Jesus, and it was freely admitted that Jesus was a good theologian as well as a moralist. One result was that a great many people began to take religion far more seriously. They saw that the church stood for a definite understanding of reality which had been lost sight of in the secular world.

I have found that something like this first course is desperately needed by people today. I have seen pastors and laypeople alike liberated when they realized that there is just as much reason to value their religious experience as the evidence of their senses. Because of this need I wrote the book *Encounter with God*, which covers much the same material and can serve as a study guide for those who are ready to see that Jesus' world view is far from outmoded. This book was included by the Religious Book Club as the first selection in *A Charismatic Reader*. A teaching guide has also been prepared which can be used with it. I know of no other attempt to place experiential Christianity within the context of critical modern thinking so that the average layman might see the value of his religion in the total framework of his life.

Besides this first class, one other was required of every adult who wanted to do any teaching in the program. This was a training course in listening to people, based on the approach and practice of Carl Rogers. The purpose was twofold. Individuals were helped to understand that the first step in real love is wanting to know all about the other person. Then, by learning to lay aside their own reactions for the moment, they found that listening in a creative way to another person can be learned, and that this is the beginning of real love. *Here the very process of education became the content.*

After this there were classes using many of the great thinkers in religion from Teilhard de Chardin to Martin Buber, from Tillich to C. G. Jung. Individual books of the Bible and works from other religions were studied. Groups were formed to pursue an interest in healing prayer. A class for people over sixty-five brought the impact of the program to men and women who have sometimes been considered beyond education. There were classes in Jung's theory of personality types, his understanding of archetypes, in the Christian use of yoga, and in creative dance. Groups were formed to pursue other special interests. No subject of interest was beyond consideration.

One great plus in using the seminar method is that this way of teaching creates teachers. Those who become most deeply involved in the classes are soon able to conduct a class themselves. The advantages are apparent. If, say in a two-year period, one teacher can touch ten people deeply enough so that five of them will become teachers, and those five are then able to do the same, the effect of the program can grow in geometric progression. From this kind of base a solid Christian venture can grow.

The need for comfortable and adequate facilities for Christian education is sometimes overlooked. When we began the program of classes, selecting attractive furniture and decoration for the classrooms went along as one part of the content. If a church does not consider such a program important enough to provide the proper setting, then the church simply lets people know that its Christian education is not truly important. The place of meeting is sacramental of what one is doing in it, and the kind of surroundings will produce an unconscious reaction which can either add value to the program or devalue what is going on. It is difficult to communicate the idea that Christianity is the most important thing in the world if we do not provide quarters which reflect this conviction.

There is one problem in the seminar method. Seminars are not encounter groups. Their purpose is to use the group dynamic process to facilitate education. But when people are given the freedom to express themselves, their deepest concerns and fears and problems often emerge. A class is usually not the best place to deal with these concerns. It is up to the group leader, first, to be strong enough not to allow such problems to swamp the group and disrupt it, and then to be available for individual discussions with any members who do become troubled and upset. It is even more important to have professional resources available so that people can be referred for counseling when problems emerge that need to be dealt with.

Our own experience was that almost half of the people who had experience in the class groups went on into individual counseling. If the church is truly a healing place, there can be no better place for the individual to find his concerns and fears and neuroses coming into the open and begin to deal with them. We were fortunate to have teachers who were secure enough so that these things did not threaten them, and to have established relations with counselors who had the insight to carry on from where the classes had to leave off. Over the years, it was clear that the greatest growth in Christian wholeness usually came to those who used both the group experience of Christian education and the individual experience of counseling as well. Each adds a dimension of growth that is difficult for either one to approach alone.

Perhaps the biggest reason for the failure of the Christian education program of the Episcopal church which used the Group Life Lab and its group dymanics was that it provided no place to refer those who had been opened up by the group process. They went back to Georgia or western Nebraska, or wherever, and with no one to help them with what had emerged things soon stopped moving again. The interaction of a group that reaches any real depth opens people to what has been successfully repressed. If Christian education is to make a dent beyond the top layer of cerebral gray matter, it must have facilities to deal with whatever is hidden within the individual life which can either hinder or promote its Christian growth.

A Program for Children

Most people think of Christian education as beginning and ending with children, and yet we have scarcely mentioned children until now. This does not mean that they were left out. One immediate result of the program was that adults who were parents began to respond in a different way to their children. As the parents changed, the children changed too, and in the most natural way. They picked up new ideas and attitudes as a part of their living environment. As research has shown, this is the way the religious and moral ideas of children are normally formed. The influence of parents, particularly of the mother, far outweighs that of other significant adults like teachers or recreation directors.

In addition to this, a new kind of program for children was developed in the church. We called it the Vanguard Program. It was offered on Wednesday afternoons because we recognized that many families in a suburban area are away on weekends. The requirements for regular attendance were the same as for the adult classes. Each class was limited to eight students; each had two teachers who worked with the group for an hour and a half. The effort was to establish group interaction, involving the children so that their needs and interests could be met and touched. The material introduced was usually in the form of examples and symbols that seemed simple outwardly, but which could be used to compare the child's experience with what men have learned and expressed about God.

The materials were often extremely simple—water was poured from a pitcher into each child's cup, which could be called half full or half empty; in a darkened room each one lit a candle from a large candle placed in the center of the group. Children are naturally open to the spiritual world, and the aim was to bring confidence in the loving quality of that world as it was opened up in the life and resurrection of Jesus Christ. They quickly grasped the idea that all of them had had experiences that were essentially religious in nature, and that they knew stories from the Bible that told of similar things. They learned to talk about these experiences, and then to pray together. Many of them began to study the Bible on their own and to ask about it. and about themselves.

Since the teachers had dealt with their own experiences and

had a place for the occurrences described in the Bible, they were able to be open and offer the youngsters support by their answers. As their religious attitudes were encouraged, the children became increasingly secure and searching in their questions. Again and again teachers remarked on the close similarity of the experiences they brought to those described by Frances Wickes in *The Inner World of Childhood.* Because the children were treated as individuals in their own right, their natural attraction to Christianity (to use Tertullian's famous phrase) was allowed to develop. For most of them this hour and a half was the high point of the week.

At the same time services and classes were provided for the parents who brought children to the Vanguard classes, and they too began to realize that Christian education was important, more important than dancing classes or tennis lessons. Later we had Vanguard classes on Sunday mornings as well as on Wednesdays. For the teachers, in addition to their weekly preparation, there was a two-hour seminar each week with the leader of the program, and later with another person who had been trained in the program. Here they brought their successes and failures, tapes of their classes, and materials and ideas to share. Most important they learned to communicate with each other, for adults who cannot communicate with each other are not likely to communicate in depth with children.

Gradually classes were made available all the way from pre-school through junior college. The preadolescents and adolescents were taught by teachers with considerable training in the ideas of Christianity and the group process, who were not troubled by the doubts and questions of these young people. Indeed they were encouraged. The classes were places where the young people could express any feelings or attitudes or ideas they wished about religion and the religious establishment and about life in general. They were particularly impressed by the basic material of the beginning adult class, and material presenting the same world view was provided for this age group. They were quick to see its significance for their own religious quest.

One important part of this program was to remodel and refurnish all the children's quarters. The church school buildings had been designed originally so that children could be introduced to religion in large groups, and these larger quarters were cut down into smaller rooms and attractively painted. Inadequate smaller buildings were torn down and replaced with modern classrooms. How often Dr. Backus reminded me that it was one thing for Christian education to take place in inadequate facilities when nothing better was within the reach of the families concerned. But children are much more perceptive than we often think. If money and effort are spent on their homes and schools, but not on the rooms they go to at church, they realize very quickly what is important to their parents and the community. Unless the church facilities are at least as adequate as their homes, religion is likely to take second place.

One section of the buildings was remodeled to provide a setup for learning to listen to children. A microphone and a mirror giving one-way vision were placed between two playrooms. In one of them a child talked with a teacher especially trained to respond to whatever the child wanted to talk about, always with a trained supervisor listening and observing from the other room. A class of adults was then brought in with the supervisor to learn ways of listening and responding to children. The sessions with the child lasted for half an hour, followed by a period of adult discussion. There was nearly always a waiting list of children for this program as long as it continued. Many of the adult listeners expressed their gratitude for the program. By listening to other people's children, they were far better able to listen to their own and found new levels of relationship with them.

Results

Although the original leadership is gone, much of the same program still continues. In addition, its basic ideas have been spread from place to place by those who were involved in it, simply through course material they took with them or remembered. Today there are people who went through the program who are deeply involved in similar efforts—either as lay people, clergy, or clergy wives—in at least twenty other parishes. Ministering to a congregation in California is like ministering to a parade. While this has its frustrations, it does provide good seed carriage to other places. This program has been the inspiration for numbers of others like it.

The fact that it has carried to other places without a formal layout tells something of its effectiveness. Hundreds of letters have come to the church expressing thanks for the program. Adults have found their Christian foundations. Young people have found that a church with wisdom can care and be comfortable with them, and children were made more solid in their Christian faith and experience. One of the reasons I was asked to teach at the University of Notre Dame was because of things I learned in the program which Ollie Backus conceived and which we implemented and supported together. It was also in this way that I learned the value of the seminar as a teaching tool.

Dr. Backus and I both felt sure that Christianity cannot be communicated without a solid intellectual foundation. As we worked, each from our own point of view, to formulate this base and make it available to people, we found our understanding confirmed again and again. Others began to realize the depth and complexity of human nature that one finds revealed by Jesus of Nazareth when one listens to his teachings in the depth that is there. They saw that Dr. Backus brought a knowledge and expertise in the educational process which put these elements together in usable form, and they worked to acquire some of the same skill.

Can Christians be educated? The answer we found is an unqualified *yes*. The problem is that it takes an earnestness and sincerity which few of us put into our Christian action, particularly our Christian education. Beyond this it requires three things. First, the Christian educator must be able to beat the secular world at its own game and show man that he is in touch with a spiritual reality. Second, Christian educators must know in their own experience that the creative victory of the Risen Christ is still available in the world of spirit to those who turn to him, and this means developing the inner way which takes as much training as for any profession. Finally, they must know the dynamics of how human beings function individually and in groups. With this knowledge they can bring the love of Christ into concrete action in individual encounters and group meetings.

Depth psychology offers real help in each of these steps. But in itself depth psychology is neutral. It can be used to increase separation and hostility and the power of the leader, as in the Hitler youth groups. Or it can be used to bring fellowship, understanding, and the giving of self in order to facilitate our loving one another as Christ has loved us. This is not very different from the way a knowledge of medicine or agriculture can be used to alleviate human misery, or only for profit and power.

Christianity can be communicated. Christians can be taught. But the process costs real effort and hard work. It also means taking the risk of suggesting this kind of commitment to nominal church members. Usually it has been the persecuted church which has transmitted the Christian faith most effectively. Perhaps the time has come for Christians, persecuted or not, to put the same effort into spreading the Christian life. In fact, real Christianity may well be more persecuted by the ridicule and indifference of today's world than we have realized. This needs to be changed, and the change can come through personal devotion to a careful, thoughtful program.

We turn now to the most essential elements of such a program. Just how such a program is arranged, what materials are used to present various subjects will depend upon the preferences and abilities of the individuals who become teachers. This is one of the reasons for a trained director who has the psychological insight to help individuals develop their strengths in a variety of ways. For this reason I shall not attempt to deal with the education of children, which requires the joint creativity of leader and teachers to present what the adults have learned in a form suitable for each age group.

We shall look first at the need to introduce people to the practice of Christianity through education in prayer and in demonstrating love or *agape*. Next we shall consider the central problem of this kind of education, that of learning the process of communication, learning *how* we can communicate these essential practices to others. We shall then turn our attention to the individuals who are trying to communicate this religion of ours and their necessary goals of seeking to become whole, to understand human personality and people's emotional reactions, particularly their own, and how this can lead to finding creativity and value. Finally we shall look at the world view which makes this kind of education possible, showing some of the reasons for presenting this understanding of the world as the basis for learning about Christianity.

First of all, then, how can Christians learn to use prayer as a way of finding relationship with God?

2

Education in Praying

"You must love the Lord your God with all your heart, with all your soul, and with all your mind. This is the greatest and the first commandment. The second resembles it: *You must love your neighbor as yourself.* On these two commandments hang the whole Law, and the Prophets also" (Matthew 22:37–40).

One of the strange things about modern Christians is the offhand way they treat this only basic law given us in the New Testament. They worry far more about people's belief in God than about love of God, and social and political surveys try to estimate the number of "believers" among various groups. But very little is said about our need to use prayer as a way of coming to *know* God well enough to find out whether we love him or not.

There are indications, of course, of a change in direction. The recent emphasis on "born again" experiences and the widespread interest in the experiences of other religions—like those of Zen, yoga, and Sufiism—suggest that people are looking for ways of knowing God. Even so, the search does not seem to get beyond first base very often. It usually ends either in an experience that cannot be described or communicated, or else in going back to the Bible as *the one* source of knowledge of God. The objective of continuing to find our own experiences through prayer, using the Bible as guide, tends to disappear, and the idea of coming to know God as a person is put away once more—like a statue in its proper niche, or a concept solidified in the right words.

Love, on the contrary, comes with knowing a person through many different experiences. In the next chapter we shall consider quite a bit about the ways human beings can find such experiences with each other, and in some ways there is not too much difference from prayer. In either case, for instance, one must learn to listen to the other so as to hear what is actually being communicated. But obviously it is not easy for us to communicate with the central meaning, the central force in the universe. If relationship with that meaning is as important for our lives as the New Testament and the practices of the early church make it appear, then we need to learn all that we can about the way the early Christians listened and found this relationship through prayer.

For a long time this emphasis remained alive in Christian cultures. One of the telling marks of a committed Christian was this kind of prayer life. Even after Christianity was made the official religion of the Roman state and the faith became diluted, this emphasis was not lost. Wherever monasteries grew up, the prayer life remained vital and central. Monastic groups continued to provide this emphasis for Catholics until our own century, while in Eastern Orthodox circles the same tradition is still at work. Yet present-day Christians seem to forget how important this understanding of prayer was for the spread of Christianity and for the education of those who wished to become "followers of the way."

These men and women who left their mark on all of Western civilization knew how to pray imaginatively. They took the instructions and the example of Jesus of Nazareth seriously. In practically all of his teaching Jesus used images. He taught his followers to pray to a Father who cares for his children and to address God as one would speak to his own father within the family, as *Abba*. Again and again he showed them his own need to stay in direct contact with the Father in heaven, and he reinforced that example with dozens of images illustrating that God's "kingdom"—the "kingdom" of heaven—is a reality which can be experienced here and now. Thus it was natural for his followers to pray in this way, and as they realized more and more fully the divine nature of Jesus himself, their prayer life and their understanding of reality deepened. And this unquestionably gave them power to heal and convince the skeptical pagan world.

This understanding of prayer is like an unknown foreign language to Christians today. In fact, prayer is anything but central or vital to most modern Christian life. Not only have most people become so dependent upon other cognitive faculties that they have forgotten how to use imagination, but few of them see any reason to give prayer a central place in their patterns of action and behavior. First of all, we need to look at the underlying causes of our difficulty with praying and why it is so hard for most of us to grasp the possibilities of a prayer life. Then we can examine in depth the use of images in praying, and finally ask whether it is possible for Christians to educate others in this kind of prayer life.

The Trouble About Praying Is...

Probably the main reason so many Christians have trouble with any kind of prayer life is the fact that so few sophisticated people see how praying could bring one into contact with anything beyond the space-time world. Most Christians seem to doubt that God or any other spiritual reality can actually be encountered by men. And so prayer has become little more than communing with the depths of one's self, or perhaps poetic musing about nature. With a belief like this, we are not likely to find praying as important as it was in the earlier, more vital days of Christian life. In fact, this belief is a good way of cooling our ardor for prayer. If there is nothing that can be reached beyond ourselves, why make such a big thing about it?

Why is it so hard to believe that prayer can bring experiences of God and his meaning and direction? The difficulty is not really lack of evidence, as I have tried to show in my book *Encounter with God*. Although this is too big a subject to explore in depth at this point, I shall outline briefly the background of our problem and mention the areas in which a new outlook is developing.

The difficulty is that we have lived too long encased in the picture of a universe that is purely physical and self-contained.

The positivistic scientists of the last century convinced most people that the only realities were things that could be explained in material terms and understood rationally. The theologians were no exception, and so Christian theology went through a brainwashing from which it has only begun to recover. We have been inflicted with the dogma that everything about human existence can be explained on the basis of natural order. Whether it is called "divine order" or simply the laws of nature, this makes the universe into a closed system. There is no way that God could break through into our lives in visions or dreams, through prayer, healing, miracles, or in any way that would disrupt his natural "law."

The leading scientists today are not so certain about their ability to understand man and his universe. When Robert Oppenheimer addressed the American Psychological Association in 1955, he pleaded with the psychologists not to formulate their thinking on the model of nineteenth century physics, because this is a model which physical science has already rejected. He would have told the theologians the same thing about prayer if they had been sharp enough to ask him to speak.

The men whose thinking has shaped modern science see their "laws" as only tentative hypotheses on which to build. These scientists themselves say that they do not arrive at final knowledge of the essence of things. Instead, their "laws" are like sketchy road maps of physical reality. They help us understand and get around in the physical world, and they include discoveries which cannot be understood simply on the basis of cause and effect. As Werner Heisenberg—one of the greatest of modern physicists—has put it, the natural language which speaks of things like *God* and *soul* probably comes much closer to stating the nature of reality than any of the exactly defined physical terms like *mass* or *inertia*.

Nor is physics alone in suggesting that we live in a mysterious and largely unknown world. Psychosomatic medicine, the mathematics of Albert Einstein and Kurt Gödel, the evolutionary theory of Teilhard de Chardin and Loren Eiseley, and the depth psychology of C. G. Jung all lead to the same general conclusion:

There is no good reason to deny that other factors than physical ones exert an important influence in human life. On the contrary, each of these sciences turns up bits of rebellious evidence that defy the law and order ordinarily expected in physical things. And, each of these facts gives a fresh hint of some purpose other than physical nature or man himself—and greater than either one—at work in our world.

The result is that science itself—often indirectly, but none the less firmly—proposes the hypothesis that there *is* a reality beyond this world with which man may be in communication. Once this possibility opens up, it becomes necessary to take a new look at prayer. Prayer is the way, par excellence, of communicating with this reality. The positivistic approach to science can no longer intimidate us into believing that this understanding of prayer is false. The fact is that prayer, by offering an opening to this other reality, can bring creative and transforming experience with very real, practical results.

A second basic reason for turning away from prayer is that many people have reacted to the structured and collective prayer life which they experienced with religious communities or in religious school situations. Many of us have been reacting against practices in which we were indoctrinated, practices that often verged on superstition, and were enforced by collective, authoritarian means. We have felt the need for individuality, and in seeking freedom and a basis for critical understanding of our religion, we generally forgot to sort out some of the valuables and take them along. Actually, most of us let the problem of bad communication obscure the fact that a valuable reality was being left behind. We could not see that what bothered us was more in the educational process than in its content. Each person has to examine himself to discover whether he is one who was in such a hurry to get away that he left his prayer life behind.

For many centuries there was an overemphasis on the vertical aspect of the individual's religious life. The stress was almost entirely on one's personal and individual relationship with God in his aloneness, and this put the purpose of prayer in a false light. Jesus did not describe his followers as people who grew calluses on their knees praying. Far more to the point, he said that they were people who loved one another as he loved them. Of course it is difficult for us human beings to maintain balance, but this understanding—which Jesus made clear—can bring the extremes in our prayer life into balance.

Christianity at its deepest and best has stood for both a vertical thrust towards God, and a horizontal one towards one's brother. To gain either one we do not need to abandon the other, but rather we should be caught in the tension between the two. Once we realize that there is a good test for real prayer, and that it is up to us to keep a check on whether our genuine concern for others is increasing, there is not much danger that we will quit praying. Offering real relationship to others with love requires the help that can be found in prayer, and it is important to keep an eye on our interest in praying. There is no need for it to flag simply as a reaction to the onesidedness of our prayer education.

Real prayer, prayer that reaches the depth of the individual and out beyond oneself, takes time and hard work. No other human activity requires more effort. Discipline, however, is not the most easily attained of human habits. This is probably the reason it was so thoroughly imposed within the religious communities. Without such an authoritative structure, few individuals attained to it. Everything in our mechanized and supercharged modern existence seems to militate against quiet and turning inward. It is hard to stand against the collective pattern of busy-ness, but the amount of quiet a man needs is a good measure of how much soul he is using, to paraphrase Kierkegaard.

Thinking in Images

There is another very important reason why prayer often seems meaningless and ineffectual to Christians today. It is because they bring only a part of their being to the prayer process. We have been so convinced of the value of rationality and consciousness in human beings that we forget there is any other aspect of human personality. Yet this consciousness in us is backed up—and sometimes opposed—by an active emotional life on one hand, and also by a very full inner life which we call "the unconscious," mainly because we know so little about it. And one of the principal ways we distinguish these parts of our being is by the way their activity is communicated to consciousness, by the way we know and "think" about certain things.

Where rational consciousness deals in concepts and ideas, our inner lives and our emotions, or affects, are generally presented to our conscious minds directly in images. Thus rational, cognitive thought, thinking which is just in the head, brings only a part of the human being into play. In recent years educators have become very aware of this; the teacher who uses only rational, cognitive tools does not reach his students as well as educators who use affect and images. One of the most daring and perceptive philosophers of science, Paul Feyerabend, has even suggested that scientific discovery is more the result of educated imagination than of purely rational thought. If this is true of getting to know the physical world, how very true it must be when it comes to knowing the spiritual one, particularly through prayer.

Is it any wonder that prayer which comes only from the intellect is thin and lifeless? It brings only one part of the man into the process, and perhaps the less important part at that. Such prayer cannot help but turn towards outer things, leaving the world of spirit largely untouched. Let us picture, by means of a diagram, why this is true. Let us represent the whole of man's nonphysical being by a triangle, with the tip representing the conscious portion reaching out into the physical world, and the larger, unconscious portion almost entirely surrounded by the spiritual world. Much of the time man has to keep his whole being directed towards the physical world. He has to live in this world, and to learn about it takes a total effort. To experience and deal with the spiritual world means switching directions. It means ignoring the constant bombardment of physical sensations, as best one can, and turning one's whole being towards that other world. The *un*conscious, the unknown and emotional areas of one's being are called into play. They are being asked to get into the act with consciousness, even briefly, and it is through imaginative thinking that this is possible.

What I have learned about the use of images and emotions in the devotional life did not come from any theologian or teacher of prayer, but rather through a psychologist interested in helping human beings deal with their confused and disturbed emotional life. Dr. C. G. Jung had discovered that, when he allowed

A Model or Scheme

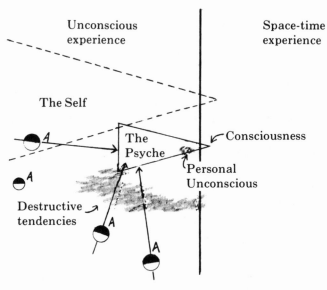

The elements of the spiritual world, or the unconscious, which affect our psyches directly are represented on the left of the central line. There are archetypal forces which can work for good or for evil in our lives depending on how we deal with them. In addition there seems to be an ultimate force for good—the Self or the Holy Spirit represented by the large triangle—and also a destructive element which is ultimately evil, shown below the psyche. These elements appear to be as real as anything we encounter in the physical world.

his own emotions to be expressed in images, they could be dealt with creatively. As he had learned from working with dreams, this is the way the unconscious does its thinking—in images and symbols. The images of dreams are typical statements of the unconscious, and this imaginative thinking may well be—among other things—a necessary step in rational thinking.

But, more important, Jung also discovered that, if one stayed in contact with the unconscious, it could be encouraged to awaken creative, helpful images which could counteract the dark, threatening ones of depressed or agitated moods. And this could bring an actual change, a transformation in the psyche. The same method, he found, could be learned and used by his patients, with the same results. He realized that this practice, which he called active imagination, was similar to the practice of Christian meditation. In fact, when I asked him what other school of psychological practice was closest to his own, he made this quite clear. Instead of naming one psychological group or another, he answered, "The classical Christian direction in nineteenth century France, under men like Abbé Huvelin." Here the kind of prayer we are discussing was used.

Praying in Images

Once one entertains the possibility that man is a bridge be-tween two worlds, then his use of images can open his inner life to reality which can become known to his conscious mind. This other, nonphysical reality—once it has been perceived and grasped—can then be understood in much the same way as our experiences of physical reality. We can use the same directed, cognitive reasoning to help us analyze and understand our ex-periences of it.

This understanding of another reality is the basic principle of *The Spiritual Exercises* of Ignatius Loyola. Certainly no prayer practice has been more effective over the last four hundred years. Individuals are taught here to hold an image up before their consciousness—the image of the Christ, of the Virgin Mary, the cross, the resurrection. By doing so, they then become open to the spritual reality which these images picture and symbolize. At the same time they will find emotion awakened within them, and this has two results. A person not only comes into contact with spiritual reality itself, but knows it in a new way; the contact is enriched by the emotion it arouses. And since emotion is one of the most effective agents of religious change, it also works to change the individual from within. It is interesting that when emotion is highly charged, ESP phenomena frequently occur. People then seem to be the most open to telepathic and psychokinetic happenings.

All through the Christian centuries such practices have been common among the masters of the devotional life. These men and women have sought to open themselves to the depths of their own being so that in this way they would come to experiences of the actual spiritual world. When it is understood that the images of dreams and visions come from beyond the borders of personal life, then these images can become windows or stepping-stones into another reality. Once they are understood to represent this reality, then they can be allowed to move, simply to "happen," absorbing one for a while almost like an absorbing novel. And in much the same way the images and stories of the Bible, especially those told about Jesus and by him, can be used to give access to this reality. Meditative or contemplative use of scripture is one kind of prayer.

If the New Testament actually does describe a breakthrough of spiritual events into the space-time world, then these events are not limited by time. By living them imaginatively, one can be brought into actual contact with the reality which broke through then, and is still available now. Various events of Jesus' life can be allowed to live—for instance, the raising of Lazarus, the transfiguration, or the quieting of the storm on the sea of Galilee. One can use the resurrection appearances, the crucifixion, or indeed any of the happenings in the life of Jesus. Or, as the early church fathers so often did, one can allow the parables of Jesus to move in the same way.

There is no need to pull back for fear of finding meaning in the stories besides a familiar one. If Jesus really was the incarnation of God—as our faith suggests—then his coming, the things he said and did, were not meant for just one group living in one particular time. They must certainly have several levels of meaning. The record itself suggests that God did not give a carefully worked out, cognitive system of salvation. Instead he spoke to various ones in various ways. To the prophets he spoke in images, in visions and dreams. Then he came as a man, in the most concrete of images. Indeed, the person who prays in this way, and experiences something breaking through, is likely to find that he is more sure than ever about the incarnation of God in Jesus.

When Jesus taught his disciples to pray, he did not use words for God like "ground of being," or the "absolute," or the "eternal nameless one." He used just plain *father*. He suggested that we hallow his *name*, and ask that his *kingdom* come so that we may be helped to do his *will*. He taught us to pray for daily *bread* and forgiveness of *debts*. He told us to ask the "father" not to put us to the *test*, and to deliver us from the *Evil One*. His prayer is nearly all in images, and he illustrated what he meant about the kingdom of God in the most concrete terms. How different this is from the idea of many people that God will not understand them unless they address him like a professor of logic, in carefully worded concepts.

In the Greek Orthodox tradition, imaginative prayer was reinforced by the use of icons, the characteristic images of Greek devotion. The icon is a religious painting, picturing some saint or a scene from the life of Jesus, executed within a carefully defined tradition. It is seen as a window into eternity or heaven. This understanding of works of art probably goes back to Plato, who considered artistic works a product of "divine madness," inspired directly from the realm of ideal, mythical reality. Whatever the tradition, great art does reveal and establish connections with the nonphysical world. This is apparent in great church art, as in the Cathedral of Chartres or in San Vitale in Ravenna, where one finds himself open to a deeper dimension of reality. It is also true of such great works of Christian literature as Dante's *Divine Comedy*, which piles image on image to carry one into the midst of that other reality of the Christian message. Again, for the Navajo Indian, it is much the same relation of art to prayer which gives Navajo sandpainting its healing power.

Images have been used in other ways in the religions of many peoples. In shamanism, which is found in so many places, every phase of the shaman's life, from initiation on, involves working with images and meditating on them. Numbers of people have been made aware of these practices by Carlos Castaneda and his works of popular anthropology. In several books he describes how his teacher, Don Juan, led him through ritual and meditation to know spiritual reality in apparently very concrete images, and to realize that these realities affect us all. Once he was aware of them, he had a chance of dealing with this reality. By becoming one who could *see*, he could then become a warrior.

On the other hand, Eastern religious practice, which is attracting many young people today, has a different emphasis. It stresses the discipline of body and emotions as a way of freeing one's self from the illusion of maya and egocenteredness. Yoga, for instance, emphasizes control of breathing as one bodily function which can be controlled both consciously and unconsciously, and this has a profound effect upon emotion and imagination. One who practices either yoga or Transcendental Meditation expects a flood of images, but the purpose is simply to let them come, and go beyond them to an experience of God without form. One may also pray with an image—expressed by a sound, a name (or mantra), or perhaps a mandala (a perfectly balanced drawing)—but his effort is to rise above other images, not to deal with them.

The Use of Images Today

The movements of New Thought starting with Phineas Quimby, Science of Mind, and the various schools of positive thinking all stress the importance of using images in "positive thinking prayer." In Claude Bristol's book, *The Magic of Believing*, we find this point of view carried to the point of magic. (I can almost *hear* eyebrows go up.) But the important thing is that this kind of praying works. People use it and find results. This use of images not only channels one's energy; it seems to tap resources beyond the individual as well. When destructive and self-annihilating thinking is replaced by creative and hopeful thinking, the structure of the psyche begins to change and one becomes open to a more positive aspect of reality. Of course, this is not all of prayer, and this kind of praying often has no place for sacrifice and suffering. But simply because there is more to it than this is no reason for avoiding a kind of prayer that is needed.

Many people who pray for the sick find that it is not nearly as effective just to state in words that healing is needed, or to frame the concept that God desires healing for the sick person. As many of us have learned through Agnes Sanford, this is only half of the job. By calling up an image of the diseased part and seeing, for instance, light flood into it, one becomes more deeply involved in the process of praying, and things happen. Mrs. Sanford has described this practice well in *The Healing Light* and in her novel *O, Watchman!* People involved in the Pentecostal movement often find that images come to them which have the greatest meaning.

Jung's description of the psyche helps to show why this is true. When the whole person is involved in the process of praying, elements of nonphysical reality are called up, divine elements, which can reach out and awaken similar elements within the other person. As the prayer group with whom I met for years found, this kind of imaginative prayer takes time. One cannot summon images in a hurry. First of all, one must take the time to become quiet, and then allow images to flow, seeking those which can bring our emotional life into harmony with our intention. It is often easier to do this with a group who are seeking in the same way. Each individual psyche can be deeply touched and brought into the silence, and then into the imaginative frame of reference. The group process actually helps some people become open to this kind of experience.

There is another, even more important fact. This kind of praying awakens us to the reality and depth of the world of spirit with which we are surrounded. It gives each of us a way of dealing with this reality, and of opening ourselves to its creative aspects rather than being stuck in the destructive elements. Once one has encountered the creative, victorious, risen Christ as a cosmic reality, then he is usually more open for the Christ to act in and through him again and again. And this is what prayer is all about: becoming open to the reality of a loving God and allowing that Reality to act through one's actions and prayers. Praying in images is one important step in the realization of this goal.

Can This Way of Prayer be Taught?

It is my experience that nearly everyone can learn this way of prayer once there is a real desire to seek knowledge of the spiritual world. For quite a few years I have worked in this way with individuals, with prayer groups, and with a great many people in seminars and conference groups. I have also seen many individuals work with Jung's technique of active imagination, which includes several of the essential elements of imaginative prayer. In many cases I have been able to observe the changes in the lives of these people. Most of those who made the effort were able to work with images to at least some extent, and so found contact with the spiritual realities that are awakened to consciousness by images.

My own experiences of the life of prayer led me to write about it for others in my book *The Other Side of Silence: A Guide to Christian Meditation*. In this study I have tried to discuss most of the ways of becoming open to the use of images in prayer, and these are also the ways of helping other people find the deepest experiences of prayer of which they are capable.

If one wants to educate others in this classical Christian way of praying, the first task is to be very sure of one's own experience of prayer. Our own convictions about the reality of the spiritual world and our experiences of change in our own lives offer the best base for helping others discover the realities that can be encountered through images and prayer. Our own belief and knowledge and experience open up a deep well of inspiration to which we can return again and again to find new suggestions for our own lives and ones that others can try.

There are also various practices found in the Christian tradition and in the traditions of other religions which are designed to help a person become open to the spiritual world and the experiences of prayer. As I have described in *The Other Side of Silence*, they range from complex techniques like yoga or Zen to fairly simple practices such as the Jesus prayer or letting the Lord's prayer or the Hail Mary establish a rhythm of deep breathing and bring body and mind to the quiet state of meditation. Any of these ways of opening a person to images from beyond our normal consciousness can be taught and individuals can learn to use them effectively, particularly if the teaching is then reinforced by working with images in a prayer group situation.

In addition, there is specific information about ourselves and the world around us which can help to open people's understanding to the reality of the world of spirit that surrounds us, and this information can be shared and passed on to others. As I have shown in *Encounter with God*, some of the information has to do with our scientific evidence about the world and how scientific facts come to us. Another area relates to the way we use words and how our words—used unconsciously—sometimes take charge of the ideas we are trying to express. Then there are facts about the psychological problems of human beings and how difficulties like neurosis, depression, anxiety, and even physical problems can be resolved through conscious relation to the realm of spirit. These facts, of course, are closely tied to the use of images in prayer, since praying in this way offers us the best chance to become conscious of the spiritual realities that are at work within and through us.

All of this information can be taught effectively in small class groups where individuals have an opportunity to discover their own reactions to the material that is presented and can learn from things that happen in their own lives. In this situation, most people will discover the value of allowing images to arise in prayer, and thus they find a new sense of conviction about the reality of God and the elements of spirit that make up his kingdom. Praying in images, many people find, actually transforms those who pray in this way, even banishing neurosis and depression. Those who learn this way of prayer find that it is worth their while, even though it takes discipline, energy and time. As one friend remarked after study and effort to acquire this skill, "This is the beginning of Christianity in action. Prayer without images hardly made a dent in my life."

Imaginative prayer, in fact, can lead us to know and express the father's love in a way that is scarcely possible when we depend upon our own desire and will. Yet this, of course, is only part of the story of Christian action. Our own feelings, our emotions and reactions to outer circumstances, particularly to other people, keep interfering with the way we impart love to others. And this is the other, equally difficult half of what it means to be a Christian. Too often we come to feel God's love, thinking that we love God with all our heart and soul and mind, and then let that love die on the vine simply because human values and other human beings put obstacles in the way of our realizing it.

At the same time most Christians seem to be convinced that *love* is something which "just happens," and that people cannot be taught to love or acquire this elusive quality by practical learning. But this is just the point we are trying to make—that Christians can be educated, that they can be taught by very practical routes, first to find the love of God, and then to offer much the same kind of love to their fellow men. Let us turn now to the possibility of becoming educated in the way of love. We shall consider first the general idea of Christian love, and then look at some of the ways in which my own education in love took place. We shall then take stock of the various ways in which we can show love to the different groups of people who touch our lives. These are ways of beginning to "love your neightbor as yourself."

3

Education in Love

At Christmas time a friend wrote me one of the most magnificent letters I have ever received. In it he asked the question: "Why does the mystical experience, the direct experience of God, seem to fill religious history, but seem absent for most people in our time?" He then went on to write these words:

> I slowly began to think that the answer to this might be similar to many questions of like nature—that we are not so very different from medieval man or man of the time of Christ as we think. Only the form or manner of expression changes, not the essence. I think that the mystical experience, the unitive vision, is as much among us and as available as it ever has been. The finding takes only simplicity and directness. The simplicity yields that most simple statement possible from scriptures: God is love. Directness takes one to search for the experience of Love within one's own life.

What he says is indeed very simple—we can find the splendor of God only as we come to know what love is concretely, in our own lives and however it expresses itself in us. *Yet most of us are afraid truly to love....*

With love there are no defenses, and one may be hurt deeply, again and again. And then, as one truly loves, the power and majesty and splendor of God come upon one, and this is not always gentle or easy to take. The splendor of God has little in common with a Sunday School picnic, or the parlor game of "love." When one allows himself to love specifically, fully and consciously, concretely in depth, then one is at the very edge of Love itself (love with a capital L), almost touching the mystical splendor of God. From many sources we are told that the mystical splendor of God will first burn one down, melt away all that does not belong to him, shear him of everything that he thought necessary for life, destroy everything that is not pure gold in him. This is not an easy experience. But it is the most important one in life, and probably the only human experience that is eternal and cannot be lost in the shuffle.

So often we like to talk about love, and deal with it philosophically or by writing poetry about it, when the important thing is to live it. As Laurens van der Post has expressed so clearly in his novel *The Seed and the Sower*, love has to be brought down to earth by men who exemplify and manifest it. The task of every real man, he says, is to make the universal specific, the general concrete. The job of the Christian, then, is to allow Love to act in and through him in *specific action,* in *concrete kindness and loving deed.*

The only real betrayal of life is the refusal to love. For it is this refusal that gives evil a chance to grow. By refusing to give first place to love, which unites and draws together into wholeness, evil in its true form of separation and disintegration is given a foothold in one's own life. How easy it is to find excuses not to love, to see instances which give us a right not to love, particularly when the person who needs our love is one who embarrasses us or seems unlovable. In this way we give evil a chance to live and grow in the one place where we can affirm life—in ourselves and those around us. The story van der Post tells in *The Seed and the Sower* is of just such a betrayal of life, told in so moving a way that it brought tears to my eyes. The wonder of his story, however, is in the fact (based on an actual occurrence) that the betrayal was recognized and redeemed by a concrete action of love—before it was too late!

One incident involving such positive action of love was told by Bruno Klopfer, a psychiatrist and an authority on the Rorschach test. One of his students was given the assignment of taking an experimental Rorschach on a woman who had been institutionalized in a state hospital in Colorado for five years. She had had both electroshock and insulin shock therapy. Her condition had finally been judged incurable. But the Rorschach showed some signs of life. Although the student had had no training in psychotherapy, Dr. Klopfer suggested that he return to see the woman once a week, just for a friendly visit. He saw her six times, and after the sixth visit the woman was well enough to return home. In commenting on the story, Dr. Klopfer has suggested that 50 percent of all psychotherapy is essentially the effect of loving concern, nothing more than interest in another human being—something which certainly need not be limited to the psychiatrist's office. Loving concern *listens*—of which we shall have more to say later. This concern also resists the temptation to make others dependent on us for our own need.

The value of such personal concern and interest is so great in both therapy and ordinary human relations that certain psychologists have made this conception the basis of essentially their whole point of view. Harry Stack Sullivan, for instance, put his entire stress on interpersonal relations, and Robert Leslie gave the same place to love in his view of logotherapy.

Yet so often it is difficult for us to love those who are nearest for us to love . . . our families. It is strange how we let our pride and hurtness, our ideas and feelings out of the past keep us from expressing love where it should be most expected and is most needed. Recently I came across a passage about the childhood of Origen, one of the great theologians of the early Christian church, which tells of the love his father gave him as a child, a love that probably explains something of Origen's later greatness. The story goes that each night as the child lay sleeping, the father would come and kiss the child's naked breast, for he said this breast was "the temple of the Holy Spirit and he was never nearer that Spirit than when he imprinted those kisses there." A little overdone, you say? Perhaps, but one who has not known affection as a child seldom grows into a loving person capable of independence and love.

In fact, recent studies on sex and sexuality show that even monkeys who have been treated mechanically fail to develop any love response either emotionally or sexually. One must be loved in order to love. This is clear in regard to criminals. As the chief parole officer of New York State has noted, the only common characteristic he could detect among the hardened, professional criminals with whom he dealt was the absence of deep and genuine love in the backgrounds of such people. Thus the vacuum of their lives was filled with hate, rather than love.

Philosophy, Theology, and Love

As I considered the power of love, its reality and closeness to the nature of God, I went back once more to Plato, first to the *Symposium*. Here Socrates says that Love is indeed a god, the greatest of the gods, being the only one powerful enough to control the others. There are often great truths one can learn from the simple and profound stories of polytheism. This particular truth simply bears out the reality of what Christ said. Then in the *Phaedrus* Plato went on to say that those who are inspired by Love are the greatest and most influential of men. The soul, once touched by the nature of the greater gods, cannot return to a simply earthy realm, and those who continue to develop their capacity for truly loving then become the most important people in society . . . as necessary as the philosophers, or statesmen, or poets . . . a veritable leaven of the lump. . . . How close the intuitions of Socrates and Plato come to the life and words of Jesus of Nazareth.

And then, as so often happens, I came upon the same truth in other places. Karl Jaspers, the existential theologian, I found had written words very similar to Plato's in his slender volume, *Death to Life*. Reading it for quite a different purpose, I was drawn to the statement: "The consciousness of immortality needs no knowledge, no guarantee, no threat. It lies in love, in this marvelous reality in which we are given to ourselves. We are mortal when we are without love and immortal when we love." And again, "I achieve immortality to the extent that I love . . . I dissipate into nothingness as long as I live without love and therefore in chaos. As a lover I can see the immortality of those united to me in love."

One day I was talking with a woman whose life was withering away because she had cut off her ability to love. To her it only seemed to bring trouble ... as she put it, "to bring down the wrath of God on my head." I was moved to pick up Jung's autobiography and turn to the final section of his "Late Thoughts," not really sure of his specific phrases, but only that he had spoken of a reality that was needed. Together we read:

In my medical experience as well as in my own life I have again and again been faced with the mystery of love, and have never been able to explain what it is. Like Job, I had to "lay my hand on my mouth. I have spoken once, and I will not answer" (Job 40:4 f.). Here is the greatest and smallest, the remotest and nearest, the highest and lowest, and we cannot discuss one side of it without also discussing the other. No language is adequate to this paradox. Whatever one can say, no words express the whole. To speak of partial aspects is always too much or too little, for only the whole is meaningful.

Love "bears all things" and "endures all things" (1 Cor. 13:7). These words say all there is to be said; nothing can be added to them. For we are in the deepest sense the victims and the instruments of cosmogonic "love." I put the word in quotation marks to indicate that I do not use it in its connotations of desiring, preferring, favoring, wishing, and similar feelings, but as something superior to the individual, a unified and undivided whole. Being a part, man cannot grasp the whole. He is at its mercy. He may assent to it, or rebel against it; but he is always caught up by it and enclosed within it. He is dependent upon it and is sustained by it. Love is his light and his darkness, whose end he cannot see. "Love ceases not"— whether he speaks with the "tongues of angels," or with scientific exactitude traces the life of the cell down to its uttermost source. Man can try to name love, showering upon it all the names at his command, and still he will involve himself in endless self-deceptions. If he possesses a grain of wisdom, he will lay down his arms and name the unknown by the more unknown, *ignotum per ignotius*—that is, by the name of God. That is a confession of his subjection, his imperfection, and his dependence; but at the same time a testimony to his freedom to choose between truth and error.

This woman was touched deeply by Jung's thoughts. They touched her situation in a way that today's religious thinking can rarely do. So much of this thinking, this current theology, is rooted in the introspections of two men who were never able to have a mature love for anyone. By following the ideas of Kierkegaard and Nietzsche, who were both crippled in their capacity to love, much of religion has forgotten how men are found of God, how they come to know and be known of him. Indeed when such theology examines things frankly, it can hardly avoid the conclusion that God is dead.

Nor does the rationalistic position, Thomistic or phenomenological, allow love a central place. From this point of view only rational certainty has value, and man's reason is seen as the only way to reach knowledge that is certain. Since men can reach beyond themselves only by their power of reason, there is no way that love could give access to another realm of reality, and so in this view its cognitive function is lost.

Jesus, however, seemed to think otherwise. For instance, he said:

> As the Father has loved me, so I have loved you. Remain in my love. If you keep my commandments you will remain in my love, just as I have kept my Father's commandments and remain in his love. I have told you this so that my own joy may be in you and your joy be complete. This is my commandment: love one another, as I have loved you (John 15:9–12).

If we take Jesus seriously, we must certainly take these words seriously. They are the heart and kernel of the gospel, the inner meaning of the parables of the prodigal son, the lost sheep, the good Samaritan. This was the meaning of Jesus' last words after the resurrection: "If you love me, feed my sheep." It is all of one piece. The same meaning is repeated in the letters of John, the letter of Peter where he says that love covers a multitude of sins, the letters of Paul. In Paul's writing, the words for *love* and for *Holy Spirit* are used practically interchangeably, and one may be substituted for the other without changing the essential meaning. As Paul put it, all our spiritual gifts are worth nothing without love.

One modern French scholar has added a long-range view of

this. Writing in the French *Review of Philosophy and Theology*, he commented on the amazing love among Christians, their sense of being members one of another. "If they had not had this quality," he remarked, "the world would still be pagan. And the day when this quality is no longer there, the world will become pagan once again."

What is Mature Love? (*A story: Part 1*)

Mature love seeks more to give than to receive. This insight came to me as I was flying home from a mission in North Carolina. Suddenly the words of the prayer of St. Francis, which I had not realized that I knew, came flooding into my heart and mind. I was flying almost over the homes of my brother and father. I was on my way to see my daughter. Suddenly the realization swept over me that I had been much more interested in receiving love than in giving it. My job, instead, was to be the center of caring for my parent even though he had certainly not understood me, for my brother who was a stranger, and my daughter who was just emerging from teen-age rebellion. A great deal went through my mind, but the most central were these words of St. Francis:

O Divine Master, grant that I may not so much seek
to be consoled . . . as to console,
to be understood . . . as to understand,
to be loved . . . as to love.

I realized all in a moment how much more often most of us human beings seek to be loved and understood and consoled than to reach out with consolation and understanding and love. I saw how often I had gone out of my way to have others console and understand and love me, and how seldom I had really tried to offer these responses to them . . . and this applied not just to strangers, but to my parish and even to my family. How often we parents even try to get our children to satisfy our needs for consolation and love and understanding. And how many adult children there are still trying to look to their parents for these expressions of human warmth.

How often we complain, "So-and-so did not speak to me," or "She had a party without inviting me."... "He didn't want me to be in the group, or he'd have paid proper attention to me." How often our feelings are hurt, and for a multitude of reasons, from an imagined slight to an actual cross word. How often we turn loose on another person our own reactions of fear or anger. If one takes seriously the kind of love expressed by St. Francis, and the need of every person for it, most of his complaining must cease because it is simply not so important. If one is thinking about bringing consolation and understanding to others, it is almost impossible to harbor hurt feelings himself. Once he knows the hurt and pain and fear of others, he is no longer able to think just of himself, and let loose his own fear and anger without caring.

The realization grew on me that emotional maturity actually begins when we do seek just such love... when we seek not so much to be consoled and understood as to console and to understand. The small child, really, is interested only in himself, in being loved and consoled and understood. When a person puts away childishness and becomes an adult, then a shift begins... when one wants to give of love rather than just receiving it and one begins to offer these things... this is the essential mark of the real adult.

In *The Face Beside the Fire*—another of his novels—van der Post has put the same truth in words with fresh impact. Speaking of the lives of his characters set against the background of primitive Africa, he writes: "For do we not all know, in our aboriginal hearts, that the tragedy of the individual is not so much not being loved as being unable to love, as if by some dark impediment which seems to cut us off from the full rhythm of life?" Indeed until one can give love and understanding and consolation without any strings attached, *without expecting anything in return*, one is only part of the whole person he was intended to be. No matter how physically or intellectually grown up, he is still simply an immature, emotional child.

In that moment on the plane I also realized that no one can begin to follow Jesus of Nazareth until he finds it more important to give understanding and consolation than to receive them. As we try to give up our desire to be consoled and understood and loved, then we die and something new begins to live in us. If we continue on this way, we lose our lives in order to gain them; we die and rise again, and this is the way of the cross. As we try actually to live by this one very clear prayer, the whole gospel begins to open up like a tight bud; it begins to make sense, and the way of Christ begins to come to life... in us....

The Results of Love (*A story: Part 2*)

When the plane landed in Phoenix, I met my daughter, determined that I would try to express this kind of love towards her. I was dreading this visit as much as she. I found out later that she had said, "What on earth will I do with father for five hours?" But suddenly I was seeing her as a real person, with real needs, not just as *my* child. I suggested that we go from the airport to the Arizona Biltmore. We had lunch sitting by the pool, and then we walked through the Thomas Shopping Mall. I saw how she kept looking at one yellow handbag. I asked her if she would like it. Her reply was definitely affirmative. Then I asked, "Would you like a pair of yellow shoes to match?" and her eyes brightened. We went shopping, and through those yellow shoes something of my new intention towards her carried. Our relationship has been quite different ever since. And ever since I have thought of this as "the sacrament of the yellow shoes."

But, you say, we have not yet defined love. No, we have not said what it is in rational concepts. Love is an experiential reality. One *knows* love, or he does not. For one who does not, it is no more possible to define than to explain the color red to one born blind, or the taste of crackers and blue cheese to one who has never tasted anything like that. One must experience love to know it. And if he would know God, he had best seek until he find it, because a man can never know or love God until he has known love from and to his brother.

Love can be known and described by its results, however. The life of St. Francis of Assisi, for instance, demonstrated these results. So magnetic was the power of his life that men were drawn to him until he was literally forced to found the Franciscan order just to give them some structure to follow. In less than twenty years his inspiration and actions revitalized a dormant and cynical church. And this was not done by discipline or intellect, but by the power of his love. The stories of it are innumerable, like the one of Francis' reply to a brother who asked him, "Why did God pick you?" The answer came back, "I guess he picked the humblest and most insignificant person he could find so that his glory would show through without any question."

In fact the results of love are so many and varied that we can only begin to list them. First of all, love breeds love, and this is the only way it can spread out into the world. In other words, in this world love is its own source. It cannot be reached through will or reason or understanding. It springs out of the total reality of the human being, body, psyche, and mind. Love that is merely rationally willed, and does not spring out of the heart, is really no love at all. It is only, in Berdyaev's words, "glassy Christian love" which has no transforming power. He believes that one reason for the sickness of the modern church is its attempt to rationalize love.

Love also has a cognitive aspect. It seems to usher us into another realm of reality. Again, Laurens van der Post, out of the almost incredible variety of his experience, has summarized the same thing said by Jesus, by John and St. Francis, Plato, Jung, and Jaspers.

> If there is one telling image inherited from the past that causes much fatal, cynical and ironical misunderstanding [he wrote in *The Face Beside the Fire*], it is the image of the blindness of love. If there is one thing love is not, it is blind. If it possesses a blindness at all, it is a blindness to the man and the man-made blindnesses of life; to the dead-ends, the cul-de-sacs and hopelessnesses of our being. In all else it is clear and far-sighted as the sun. When the world and judgment say: "This is the end," love alone can see the way out. It is the aboriginal tracker, the African bushman on the faded desert spoor within us, and its unfailing quarry is always the light.

Indeed human life seems to wither away and be destroyed without love. Children do not mature properly, do not learn, do not even grow if they are not loved. As van der Post described in the same novel, there is a poison we give those close to us, family or associates, if we do not love them. The person without love is not merely let down into a neutral limbo; he is actually destroyed. Of this the novelist says, speaking of a woman and the husband she had ceased to love, "Slowly she is poisoning Albert... This poison... is found in no chemist's book.... It is a poison brewed from all the words, the delicate, tender, burning trivialities and petty endearments she's never used—but would so constantly have spoken if she'd truly loved him."

The person who has never been loved seldom has a sense of real worth or value; he has little sense of security or permanence; for it is as we are loved that we can begin to treat ourselves as human. Deep in the heart of every man is the fear that no one can abide him. This is the result of our separation from God, and only as the human soul is watered with concern and love can this disfigurement within it be cleansed away and replaced by a new growth of security and self-respect.

Faith is also a product of love, and one who has never been loved seldom has faith. How can we believe that there is a God who cares and watches over us until we we learn this love from some human being and thus are given a glimmering realization of the nature of that love which dwells at the core of reality? Von Hügel in his biographical sketch of Sir Alfred Lyall remarked that it was the cold and unloving household in which Lyall was raised which made faith so nearly impossible for him. Van Hügel saw the human family with its loving environment as one instrument of God preparing men to know Him. Jung has noted that most churchmen seem to be afraid of unbelievers, although they are the very ones—the individuals who are sick because they have not known love—that the clergy need to seek out to share the security of their faith.

Courage is another result of having been loved. The really fearful, really frightened person who lacks courage to go out and take on life is simply one more individual who has never known love. Either he has never known what it is to have another standing by him, encouraging and loving him, or else the love around him has not penetrated with this quality of unassuming, firm support. Courage is seen in the actions of those who have confidence in the ultimate nature of reality, who thus step out to risk the present for the future, the proximate for the ultimate. How does one arrive at this point? By accepting the confidence and trust that spring from being loved. It is practically impossible to be courageous—*except in hostility and hatred,* which are seldom creative—unless one has known the healing balm, the psychic stuff which is love. How can one go through the dark night of the soul, through which courage often leads, unless first one is established in love?

Nor is it possible to have hope without having known the reality of love. Love gives meaning. How can one hope for good in the future, the greatest good, unless one has known something of it in the past? Without love there is nothing to look forward to, nothing to imagine as the fulfillment of love, and so there is no hope.

Strange, isn't it, that God would put into our hands such a tremendous power? By loving or not loving we become gods ourselves, for we can create or destroy, build up or tear down. How audacious God was to put in our hands the lives of those around us, and our lives in their hands.

If we love, we create, heal, release in those around us a power which seldom fails. If we do not love, we join the forces of the evil one and destroy as effectively as if we were triggering a machine gun into a defenseless crowd. If we love, we step into the circle of the very creative action of God. If we do not love, do not in our hearts go out in compassion, and show love in action, then we step into the down-draft of evil which is destroying the world we live in. What a terrible responsibility God and life put into our hands. We can either become fonts of creativity and life, or, by not loving, cauldrons of witches' brew, poisoning the lives of all we touch. It is not even a simple question of *what we do,* but in the long run of *how we do it.* After all, Satan's real fault in the old myth was that he wanted to do things more rationally and effectively than he could by continuing in the way of God's love.

Our task as Christians, then, as men truly in touch with life, is learning to love. What we need to pass on to others is not so much education about the Old or New Testaments, about proper beliefs or epistemologies, but actual love. Should not any Christian community, and our own community in particular, be a place in which just such understanding, consolation, and love are given and received, in which each of us grows deeper and deeper in our experience of these realities?

If this is so, then we should turn to some very practical questions about how we can begin to show more love, more of the spirit of which Jesus spoke, which is described as the Holy Spirit, the dove. Is it possible to learn how to love better? I suggest that it is: that as we learn to listen, and work on loving ourselves, as we learn to love our own families, we can then turn our loving experience towards the stranger and even towards our enemies. Let us see the connection with listening.

Love and Listening

Before we can love someone we must first know that person. Loving really means giving another the concern, the appreciation and understanding he needs. It is not a matter of giving what we feel like giving, or want to give, but what the other person actually needs. Love is always centered in the need of others, ministering to that need. How can we learn to give that kind of understanding and concern? Well, quite obviously, we first have to know the other person before we can minister to his need. When we try to love without first knowing the other, we are ministering to our own needs, not theirs.

The problem of many spouses and parents is that they give what they want to give, what they feel like giving, without first finding out where the other person is, and what he wants and needs. To give without first finding out about the other is not love but a kind of selfishness. Real love always goes out to the person as he is, not as we think he is or want him to be.

How does one get to know what another is like? How do we get to know someone well enough to love them? The most important way is by listening to that other person. The significant thing is — simply — *to listen*. You think that this is something

simple and easy? How many times have you listened to a friend
or spouse or parent or child for an hour without interjecting your
own ideas or wishes? How often have you been able to put aside
your own human reactions and egotism, your wants and wishes,
and listen to the other person for an entire hour? Real listening
is a difficult and demanding discipline. There are few things any
harder to do well.

There are also few things more necessary. It is impossible to
respect another to whom you have not had the courtesy to listen.
Listening shows concern for what the other person is. There can
be no love until there is at least as much respect as is shown by
listening, not just once but over and over again. So often we
assume that we know someone quite well, forgetting that they
change. To keep knowing a person one must continue to listen to
him. It is strange how often the people who are closest to us are
the very ones to whom we listen the least. Particularly within
one's own family, a study of personality can be of real help in
understanding the other individuals and how they differ from
oneself.

How seldom do we find anyone truly interested in listening to
us. Yet how much each of us yearns to become known to another
in this way as the first possibility that one might be loved. Sometimes it takes hours and hours of testing before a person can trust
another enough to open up that secret inner being which each of
us longs so much to share. . . . Yet how can anyone love me who
does not wish to hear and bear with me the deepest and most
difficult secrets of my life?

The first step in listening is to allow oneself to be silent with
another. We must be silent not only with our lips but with our
inner responses. Listening involves an active silence in which
one reflects but neither agrees nor disagrees.

One must be somewhat secure himself before he can listen.
One has to be rather unshockable, but also quite secure in
where he stands. So many people fear that the ground of their
own belief and morality may be swept away from under their
feet if they do not defend it. They dare not listen without reactions, emotional and verbal . . . as if opinion expressed with emo-

tion were a protection. It is surprising how difficult it is to listen to another without expressing one's own reactions.

Once one has listened to a person in quiet depth, and accepted his first tentative tests of being accepted, then the floodgates open. The whole human being pours out—the entire human being with his guilts and faults and sins, with his sense of hopelessness and inadequacy and loneliness, with his self-hatred and self-judgment and inner psychic pain. This is hard to bear, because it stirs up our own darkness and loneliness. One man I have known, whose business it was to listen to others eight hours a day, found that he had to get clear away for one month out of every four in order to discharge the poison he had accumulated in listening.

As one goes on listening, accepting on this level, then one is allowed to step beyond the darkness and ugliness in the other person. One is then allowed to see the beauty that resides in every soul, a beauty which most of us never dream exists in this world, let alone in another human being. It makes no difference how depraved or exemplary, how simple or sophisticated and brilliant the individual, there is a central fortress in every soul where the spirit of God himself dwells. As one touches the deepest levels of the incredible human psyche, one begins to hear strange echoes, to see lights and catch strains of the mysterious music of the Spirit of the Christ who dwells in the human soul. Such listening is prayer in the truest sense. Through it one reaches and touches this reality found within each person's soul. Sometimes I have the same sense of awe from such an experience as one may have kneeling in the church alone at night.

Those who discover such a spirit dwelling in the human psyche find that they are also able to relate to that spirit directly. But seldom do we find this ability, seldom do we hear the still small voice of God until we first learn to open ourselves to other human beings. Rudolf Steiner put it well: "Only to those, who by selfless listening train themselves to be really receptive within, in stillness, unmoved by personal opinion or feeling, only to such can the higher beings speak. . . . As long as one hurls any personal opinion or feeling against the speaker to whom one must listen, the beings of the spiritual world remain silent." In addition, one who has found such a spirit within men, seemingly the potential of all, knows that human beings are of supreme value, and no man can be treated as a thing.

Loving One's Self

One main reason for our conflicts with others and our separation from them is that we do not love ourselves. Much of our tragic human situation is the result of the failure of human beings to value themselves. The man who does not like himself poisons his relations with others. But the first reaction of most people when I make this suggestion is something like this: "But wouldn't we be egotistical and selfish if we loved ourselves? Isn't this advice just the opposite of Christianity?"

No, strangely enough the contrary reaction occurs when we really love ourselves—once we have come to terms with ourselves, have come to accept our own weaknesses and foibles and sins and guilts. Once we have come to value ourselves and genuinely like what we are in spite of the ugliness and sinfulness we find within ourselves, then we are free to like others and treat them like human beings. Once we have come to have a genuine regard for ourselves, then we don't always have to be defensive for ourselves by drawing attention to the faults of others. We don't have to protect our own egos with a shield of anger towards others. Then we are no longer worried about how others may be talking about us, for we know how we stand with ourselves, and what others say isn't going to throw us. We won't be hurt over a slight or injury because we know the other person probably didn't mean it, and even if he did, then it is just a piece of poor judgment on his part!

You see, when a person basically likes the core of his or her own being, and accepts and is securely loved by himself, or herself, then if others don't share that opinion, it simply shows that their taste is poor. Each of us has the inside story on himself. Once one has come to know and to like himself in spite of what he knows, then the uninformed opinions of others no longer bother him. And then the most wonderful thing happens: Then a person can forget about himself or herself and turn out to others and think about *them* and what concerns *them* and how *they* react. Jesus was certainly right when he said, "Love your neighbor as yourself," and implied very clearly that we couldn't love our neighbor until we had loved ourselves. Jesus touched the very heart of the problem in these words. One who cannot accept himself as he is and even care for himself, can never really care for others.

As a practical matter, then, how can we come to love ourselves? Our first task—if we are ever to accept ourselves and become free from our bitterness and rage towards ourselves and others—is to be honest with ourselves. We cannot possibly love what we do not know. We cannot love ourselves until we are honest with ourselves and see what we actually are. This is painful and difficult, but there is no other way to self-acceptance. The main reason we hate other people is that this is so much easier than to face the uncomfortable tensions of realizing that we hate ourselves. Whenever we dislike some quality in another person with real fervor, we can be almost certain that we are seeing in them something which we can't bear in ourself. Yet people do have different prejudices, and the thing we dislike the most may not bother the other person at all.

Until we can bear the pain of looking at what we are, there is no hope of our accepting and valuing what we actually are, and thus little hope of our coming to value any other person in a real way. How can one be honest with himself? There are some specific ways. We can take time out to be still just with ourselves, without any pastime or busy-ness or TV that keep us painlessly out of touch with ourselves most of the time. We can reflect on our reactions to others. We can listen to our dreams. We can talk these things over with someone we trust. Personally I find that if I don't have someone to talk with whom I trust, who can look at me objectively and see my faults and virtues, I often remain unconscious of them. There is no beginning of any real relation between two people until one is honest with himself. Only then can he hope to care for others as they are.

The next step is to realize that it is just as morally wrong to dislike, to hate and devalue, to despise and derogate ourselves as it is to have these feelings for another human being, maybe worse. And—what may come as a shock—this is exactly what Christianity seems to say. Let us put this imaginatively. We are like silly youths cooped up in a basement room of a great house. We are not good enough to share the whole mansion and so we go off into this tiny cell of self-abasement, and there we call to God to come and help us. He comes, and says to us, "Come out of this little room and inherit your vast mansion. This is only a cellar chamber, and the whole place is yours."

But we look up and say, "Oh Lord, but we are not worthy!" Then the Lord gets angry—We will see this if we will keep looking, remembering that he can become angry now and then, but not for the things we usually think. The Lord Christ is stern and says, "How dare you call unworthy the one for whom I died, to whom I come now. You have to abandon this silly attitude or creep back into your cell by yourself and stay there. I know what is worthy, and I came and died for you, and I come when any of you calls me. Come, forget that you are proud of being able to say, 'We are unworthy.' Come with me and inherit the kingdom prepared for you from the foundation of the world."

If we have no basic value for ourselves, if we persist in hating ourselves, we are politely telling God that he doesn't know what he is doing in sending his son for us. We know better than he and so we deny our faith in him. In that act lies the mystery of our faith. This is the great mystery of our Christian experience! That God loves even us and would have died on the cross in Christ Jesus *if we had been the only one.* . . . Why I don't know. But I do know that this is the way that God sees us! How dare we, then, hate this one whom God so greatly values!

Our next endeavor—if we are ever to love ourselves and be free to love others—is to have the courage to accept the forgiveness of others. Yes, I said what I meant: *to accept the forgiveness of others.* It is far easier to forgive than to be forgiven; to forgive, than to accept forgiveness. Remember the passage in the sermon on the mount (Matt. 5:23) where Jesus said that if you bring your gift to the altar and there remember that your neighbor has anything against you, then you were to leave your gift and go and be reconciled with your neighbor. He did not say, "If you have something against your neighbor, go and be reconciled with him," but, "If he has anything against you...." In other words, if you have done something to him for which you have not tried to receive forgiveness, or for which you have not accepted forgiveness, then leave your gift before the altar and go and seek it.

I once had a very close friend offend me, so much that I was deeply hurt. But I forgave that friend. Even so, something happened to our friendship. We drifted apart until one day when we were talking, I realized that he couldn't accept my forgiveness and so he had felt himself unworthy of my friendship any longer and had withdrawn from me. From that day we began to rebuild our friendship.

One has to value one's self, love one's self, in order to accept forgiveness, and in accepting forgiveness one comes to a greater measure of this self-valuing. Did you ever realize that the whole Christian church is built on those who accepted forgiveness and loved the Lord none the less? There was Peter who denied him, John who fled from him, Paul who persecuted and destroyed his church, and yet they one and all accepted the forgiveness of God and became the founders of Christ's church.

Our last effort in coming to care for ourselves is to take the chance and relate to other human beings even if they do betray us—just as Jesus did. We must come into a real relationship with others, accepting and being accepted, forgiving and being forgiven. One cannot just sit at home and come to an acceptance of one's self. This is something that is given in the interaction of human beings. One who stays apart from others can never come to love or value himself. No man is an island, and anyone who tries to be one remains less than fully human. Only as we live our lives with other human beings, only as we are accepted and accept others—in spite of betrayal and hurt and being let down—only as we have the courage to be ourselves with others, only then do we begin to love. Then we find growing within us an appreciation and acceptance of self which draw the individual towards love for one's self, for others, and ultimately to real love of God.

The essence of the situation between a psychological counselor and the counselee, between the therapist and the patient, is just this. The patient is accepted as he is, and he begins to be able to accept himself. Ideally this is what the church is for. It is supposed to be a fellowship filled with the compassion, the understanding, the love of Christ. If it really were such an accepting fellowship—rather than the handful of isolated individuals who happen to be here on a Sunday morning—then miracles would happen, and we would find far less need for psychologists. But until that time, we must often find our religion in a counseling situation.

Loving One's Family

Once we have begun to try to love ourselves, then our love can spread out to the next circle of relationships, our family and friends. This would seem perfectly obvious, but as anyone finds who listens as a marriage counselor, love is often no greater in so-called Christian families, if as great, as among today's pagans. Yet families that are short on love are spawning grounds of neurosis. In the words of one writer on the subject, "there are no panderers, procurers, and pimps so cunning and irresistible as those parents who themselves have not experienced love."

Jesus simply assumes that we will love our families, our children, wives, husbands, our brothers and parents—even as good heathens do. What he said about it in the sermon on the mount was simply: "If you love only those who love you, what reward can you expect? Surely the tax-gatherers do as much as that. And if you greet only your brothers, what is there extraordinary about that? Even the heathen do as much" (Matt. 5:46–47, NEB). It never occurred to Jesus that he should have to tell us to love those who love us. And yet, looking at Christian families today, one does not even see this much. Are Christians who do not love within their own families as advanced as the heathens and tax-collectors, the harlots and sinners of that time? Isn't it more than a little shocking to find the general run of Christian families no more loving than anyone else? How has this come about? I have a theory.

The ancient heathen was taught to love his friends and family with a burning love and to hate his enemies with a violent hatred. He worked at both. When you had a heathen friend, he was a friend forever and you could count on his loyalty until hell froze over. After Christianity became the accepted religious idea of the Western world, men were taught that they should not hate, and so they pretended that they did not hate anyone. As a result, the hatred in them dropped down into the depth of them, was forgotten and ignored in the unconscious. Thus it worked autonomously. Hatred began to come out when least expected, even unnoticed and upon one's loved ones. In fact our families and loved ones have often had the treatment once reserved for one's enemies.

Besides this, the followers of Christ were saddled with another unique idea—the idea of the quality and value of women, and also of the value of children just as children. For this reason Christian marriage and family life require a mutuality and respect which is hard for us human beings. One must be quite conscious, quite aware to get along in a mutual relationship. This differs basically from the family in which one member or another is titular head of the house, so that a structure develops which avoids the need and the stress of mutual relationship.

Carl Jung once made a pointed comment on this whole question. A friend was telling him about a certain man and what a saint he was. Jung, with a twinkle in his eye, came back, "Oh? But I would want to know his wife and children before I decided on his sainthood." We Christians, it seems, need to consider how to love our families, as well as ourselves.

My first suggestion is simply *to show one's natural and ordinary feelings of affection and love when he feels them, and not be afraid of these feelings.* So many people I know are able to express any negative or hostile feelings, but either cannot or do not show any of the positive and loving movements of the heart. In the fourth century, St. Ambrose, in a book on the duties of the clergy, gave his ministers some of the finest advice on how we can help our Christian love to grow. He wrote:

> It gives a very great impetus to mutual love if one shows love in return to those who love us and proves that one does not love them less than oneself is loved, especially if one shows it by the proof that a faithful friendship gives. What is so likely to win favor as gratitude? What more natural than to love one who loves us? What so implanted and so impressed on men's feelings as the wish to let another, by whom we want to be loved, know that we love him? Well does the wise man say: Loose thy money for thy brother and thy friend, and again, "I will not be ashamed to defend a friend, neither will I hide myself from him."

And in discussing the popularity of King David, Ambrose remarked: "Who would not have loved him, when they saw how dear he was to his friends? For as he truly loved his friends, so he thought that he was loved as much in return by his own friends." Because of his love to his friends, people put David above their own families and children.

One excellent way of showing that one loves is by simple kindness and thoughtfulness, by doing little acts of kindness and sentiment. There is no woman who doesn't appreciate a twenty-five cent bouquet of violets (or today's equivalent), nor any child who doesn't like some small gift from father or mother returning from a trip. How seldom we do even this much! In marriage counseling, I hear more women complain that they are simply taken for granted; the husband never remembers special days, never does the extra kindness. And husbands have the similar complaint, "I am nothing but a bank account." Simply stopping to think about each other and do some small act of remembrance and caring does wonders. All of us are insecure, and we all need some little display of affection and interest in us to give us value and worth—all of us. One trouble is that we get so caught up, each in our worthlessness, that we minister to no one, and so no one ministers to us! We receive only as we give in this matter of love.

Love cannot be expressed to those we love, however, without the expenditure of time. If you really care—or want to care—about someone, then you will spend time alone with that person. Time with a wife or friend in the company of others does not have the same value as time alone with the person we wish to relate to. *How often we take those we love for granted, and simply deny them the time that is needed for relationship.* Relationship can never be given in one dose like a pill or a gift.

Then, as one takes this time, he will listen if he loves. Love always desires to find out about the other person, is interested in the events of the day, the thoughts, desires, fears, even the angers of the other. If love is genuine, it cares, and caring always involves listening. As Louis Evely has put it so beautifully in *That Man is You:*

Love must express and communicate itself.
    That's its nature.
    When people begin to love one another,
        they start telling everything that's happened to them,
            every detail of their daily life;
        they "reveal" themselves to each other,
            unbosom themselves and exchange confidences. . . .

God hasn't ceased being Revelation
        any more than He's ceased being Love.
He enjoys expressing Himself.
    Since He's Love,
        He must give Himself, share His secrets,
        communicate with us and reveal Himself
            to anyone who wants to listen.

Without listening there is no communication, and without communication there is no love. How much each one of us needs to be listened to, to be found by another who could love us as we are.

One who loves will also show his feeling for the other by touch. There is something healing in the touch, something sacramental of the giving of ourselves, and more than ourselves. Usually when Jesus healed the sick, he laid his hands upon them, touched them. How important it is not to be afraid of simple human contact. One experience told me by a friend who is a psychiatrist expresses this beyond question. He had been working for a long time with a woman whose condition did not improve very much. Then one day she was so nearly well that, after a visit or two, she did not have to see him any more. Some time later they happened to meet at a social gathering. My friend studied her face quietly for a moment, and then asked, "Would you tell me? What was it that made you well? Was it anything that I did?" And with a quick smile, she told him, "Oh, I thought you knew. When my son was in the contagious ward in the hospital, and I was waiting in the corridor for news, you came by and stopped to ask. You put your hand on my shoulder, and I knew that you cared. It was then that I started to get better."

How important the touch is in conveying to others that we care about them, love them. Can you imagine two people who genuinely love each other living together and never touching one another? It is unthinkable. Such human contact is one of the simplest, yet most important ways of conveying the feeling of love and concern. This simple human affection feeds the soul.

If we really love those within the family circle, we will also stand up for them when they are subjected to condemnation from the world, or from themselves. Our acceptance and praise are much more likely to give strength, direction and solid morality, than judgment or criticism from us. So often our judgment of children is the projection upon them of our own fears and insecurities. As van der Post has put it, "One cannot just pick out what one likes in people and reject the rest. That's using people, not loving them." Particularly is this true of children as they come to the period when they must meet new experiences on their own terms. It is certainly not easy for parents when children begin to have their own ideas and to rebel against us. But this is just when they need our acceptance and love. Only by showing our love can we help them express the hostility and frustration within them so that it does not become unconscious and destructive.

I once knew two social workers who adopted two children and

tried to raise them objectively. Within a year they had to be sent back because they were incorrigible. Then the couple took two others, and this time the home was their children's fortress and, with firmness and love, they were supported in all they did. This time the children showed the affection and love they were given. Everyone needs a place where he is accepted and considered valuable whether he is right or wrong—everyone. A real friend or parent is one who is behind you whether you are right or wrong, just because he is your friend or parent. If we love one another within the family, we will be with the others no matter what they are or do. We will also express appreciation and admiration. We will find something to praise—for the world will give little enough.

These then are several ways to express love within the family. This kind of feeling and concern, loyally and persistently expressed, is necessary if we are ever to have families in which love can grow, from which our love and concern can spread out into the world. Christianity is an extension of this pagan virtue of family love, but it cannot grow until we have it there. Only when it is based upon this kind of dogged, determined, loyal expression of love within Christian families, can it keep growing beyond them.

Loving Our Employees

For several years I have been privileged to know at least one leader in industry who has tried to apply the principles of Christian love within his particular sphere of influence. He had inherited a company which made an excellent product, but in the days after World War II it was floundering. In desperation he decided to pray, and as he prayed an answer seemed to emerge out of him. There was only one way this company could be a vital success: *He must create the conditions whereby each individual could develop to the maximum of his potential within the opportunities at hand.* The message came so clearly that he seemed to have no choice; under these circumstances his company would succeed. As it served people, it would become solid and grow.

His task, as the primary influence on the organization, was to create an atmosphere in which human beings could develop and grow. He also realized that this applied not only to the employees whom he liked, or who liked him, but to all his employees.

As this man considered the idea which had come to him, he wondered how he could create such an atmosphere. The only way he saw that it could be done was to apply as many of Christ's teachings to the practical concerns of his business as possible. This would be Christianity in action, love in action. He came up with the following eleven rules or suggestions to guide his actions:

Serve those whom you expect to serve you.

Consider no man inferior, but recognize his limitations.

Lead men by action and example.

Be humble in your accomplishments.

Teach and be taught.

Attack unfairness from any quarter.

Believe that your fellowman must prosper if you are to prosper.

Seek the truth no matter who may get hurt.

Pray for God's guidance when you must make a decision affecting the life and future of any person.

Make your own decisions based on your own best judgment only after careful consideration has been given to *all* the facts.

Forgive honest mistakes where the person making the mistake is honestly self-critical. If he is not self-critical, he must learn to be or he can never successfully supervise others or develop to his best abilities.

This is quite a set of rules. In effect, it is a base for treating human beings as persons rather than as objects, as "thou" rather than an "it." The idea has been successfully tested by this company as a basis for both personal and industrial growth. Let's look at some of the implications of these rules.

First, by seeing ourselves as serving, then we will develop along with others in the group. We must look honestly at the individuals and their personal abilities, including our own—not just at the mask of their positions or comparing them with what *we* do. It is our job to examine our own actions, our own example, and try to understand the actions of others in relation to the total situation and the place they can fulfill in it. One can neither toot his own horn, nor force others into impossible roles beyond their limitations. One must teach by example and listen, watch, and learn from each individual. To do this, each must be treated as a person in his own right who can grow and develop. Most of us do not start to develop freely until we are treated in this way, by someone who wants to share his experience and knowledge.

On the other hand, it hurts the individual, as well as souring group relations, to tolerate unfairness from any member. And if we are truly fair we will want others to prosper as we are trying to. Equally, to put our own or anyone's judgment about persons or things above the truth causes unfairness, and the individuals are hurt far worse than if the facts are sought and truth is faced squarely. Who do we think we are to make our own truth? We then make ourselves more than God and reality. Indeed, how much injury and pain and misunderstanding would be avoided if we insisted on the two standards of fairness and truth. And the only place to start is by our own determination to seek the facts and to pray to God from the depth of our being whenever we must come to a decision affecting human beings. If we will seek the truth and listen to what comes in the silent recesses of the soul as we wait in quiet, we will know that we have done the best for all concerned.

Finally, when we give others the freedom to make mistakes, we give them the freedom to grow. It is mostly by our mistakes—which all of us make—that we grow and develop. To the extent that we are able to offer forgiveness, and along with it help others to understand and evaluate their own actions by our example and praise, we help them to grow to the fullness of their abilities. Without forgiveness, men and women stop growing because they are afraid to make mistakes.

These rules apply not only in this one industrial complex. They apply everywhere, to small businesses, committees, neighborhoods. Here is Christianity in action, Christ moving in our world in words and ways that we can understand. This is treating every person as having the same value and worth as ourselves. This is what Christ came to teach, for when we do treat people this way, then God is present, breaking into the human heart and becoming known in actual reality.

Most neighborhoods would be delightful to live in if these suggestions were followed in all situations. They are even good basic rules for dealing with our families, and church disagreements would be few if these basic ideas of human relationship were applied in vestries, altar guilds, and other church groups. It is interesting that these practical suggestions for expressing love come from one concerned with running a factory, rather than from a theologian or church administrator!

Loving the Stranger

As we look beyond our circle of friends and family, out beyond the neighborhood, beyond our business associates, we find the stranger, the stranger whom we pass by, and others whom we know only through imagination and the news reports. Unless we make some effort towards the strangers who daily cross our paths, our efforts towards those whom we do not know will be only hollow and artificial. To discuss these efforts fully involves the whole subject of social action, of reaching into socially and racially depressed areas to help bring about change and self respect, of relieving poverty and misery, bringing education and understanding and alleviating neurosis and depression. These areas are of tremendous importance; indeed love that does not reach out into some social arena is hardly genuine love at all. But the subject of social action is receiving wide attention at the present time, and our concern here is with the inner motivation of love which is necessary if love is to be a social virtue.

Then there is the question of our giving, which can do much to implement our care and concern for others. This is equally important for all of us, particularly for those who are unable to be active except by giving of their substance. If we give generously and with love, it can be a true expression of concern for the stranger—so long as we remember that it is the love that counts, and that without it there is no value even if one gave away all he had. Certainly one who does not give generously of his substance, and also reach out as he is able in social action, has never caught the implications of love for the unknown and the forgotten, for the stranger. So much seems to be demanded of us by Jesus' injunction to "love one another as I have loved you."

Indeed real love goes both ways; it turns towards oneself, one's family and friends, and at the same time outward, where one finds—often closest at hand—those who are lonely. There are few more devastating experiences than loneliness. Man is a social creature, and those who do not have the deepest roots within themselves literally die when they are utterly alone for any long period of time. Life ceases to have meaning, and they are prey to all kinds of diseases of body and mind and soul.

Simply being around other people does not mean that one is not lonely. The worst and most poignant loneliness is found in the rooming house districts of great cities where there are swarms of people but no relationship or meeting of person with person. It is in these conditions that we find the greatest number of suicides. Another place of great loneliness is among the very wealthy who are separated from others after they have found that most people are trying to use them and not relate to them. It is not physical pain or even psychic pain that brings the greatest misery, but loneliness. The worst treatment in prison, for instance, is solitary confinement where a man is alone with himself and his own conscience, separated out and rejected.

Some people are lonely even in the midst of families because they feel that no one could accept them if they really knew them. Thus all human relationships seem a mockery. In the best of psychological and religious counseling one of the purposes is simply to break down the barriers of this loneliness so that another may enter and bring relationship with the person, fresh air for this staleness of the soul. But there are things each of us can do, as lay people, to help relieve the heart-breaking loneliness so prevalent in modern man. We can go out to the stranger—even if he is our own brother or child—to the newcomer, the isolated, the forgotten.

The first step in loving the stranger is simply to see him. But this is not as simple as it may sound. In order to see the stranger *one must be aware enough to look beyond himself.* One must be conscious enough so that he is not thinking of himself and his circle, his own reactions and desires. It is difficult to be conscious enough to stop and notice other human beings and try to feel with them. Usually when we come into a group we gravitate immediately to our own friends and start talking about the latest thing of interest in our lives. How seldom we stop and say to ourselves: I wonder if there is anyone here who is new or a stranger or lonely. So often we are simply unconscious that anyone might need us, might like to have one of us speak with him. It never occurs to us to think about anything beyond ourselves and our small circle.

Most of the evil in this world is caused, not by wicked people, but by unconscious people—by just this kind of unconsciousness. As Jung has shown, the unconscious person follows whatever happens to pop up within him—whether it be his own impulsiveness, his bigoted cultural heritage, or a moment of charity and concern for others—without being able to tally the harm or good that might come from his actions. Indeed in certain places Jung essentially equated evil with unconsciousness. For children the vacillations of unconscious parents may be more destructive than the evil of consistently rejecting parents. Is not the same thing even more true of the stranger, who does not even exist for us when we are unconscious of him and the effect of our actions on him?

The next, also obvious step in loving the stranger is to make the first effort to reach out to him. One sees him, and then speaks or stretches out a hand; one hears about a shut-in and makes the effort to call. This first action is very hard for some people, much harder for some than for others. For introverts it takes real courage to step out and make the first proffer of friendship. Yet without it there is no possibility of breaching the walls of loneliness. And if one is rebuffed, if the other person doesn't want to speak, then that is their problem. We have made the effort. We have opened the door. And in most cases how easily a few leading questions will open another up for our listening. Where are you from? How long have you been here? What kind of work are you in? Are you married? Do you have children? What are your hobbies? Most of us are dying on the vine waiting for someone to care enough to ask any of these questions. Don't you enjoy having another person care enough to ask, and then listen?

And then comes the last step. What will we do to integrate these people we have met into our group, or some other. If friendliness is only on the surface, it can do more harm than good. It must be backed up by action—by an invitation for dinner, for a cup of coffee or to share some common interest. Then two people, who *both* need acceptance, have begun to find it.

Everywhere we run into the stranger—in our churches, on the street, in the office. If we do not discover the stranger we do encounter, how can our love be sincere for the stranger we do not know? We do best, as Christians, to follow Jesus' own words: "For I was hungry and you gave me food; I was thirsty and you gave me drink; I was a stranger and you made me welcome; naked and you clothed me, sick and you visited me, in prison and you came to see me. . . . in so far as you did this to one of the least of these brothers of mine, you did it to me" (Matt. 25:35–40).

Loving Our Enemies

And then there is the task of loving one's enemies. How preposterous this demand of Christianity seems. How can one love when he doesn't love? How can one love the very person he hates, who angers him? Isn't one being a hypocrite to try to love when he feels anything *but* loving? Far from it. Christ tells us that we can grow in our love only as we work at it. From the experience of people who have tried to work at it, I offer six positive steps that can help us grow in actual love and in our capacity for loving.

To start on this task one must take an absolutely necessary first step. This is to recognize honestly that at present one doesn't register very high in the scale of Christian love. Not only are there people we don't like very well, but we don't even show an unrelenting love towards those who are close enough to us to expect it—our wives or husbands, our children and parents, friends, and neighbors! It is really rather shocking how little love we consistently show to those around us. Until we realize how little love we have in our hearts and lives, how little comes out consistently in action, we don't even realize that certain people are our whipping boys and certain others are studiously ignored or avoided (which can also be an expression of hatred).

There can be no growth in Christian love until we see how little of it there is in most of us, and then decide lamely and reluctantly to try to do better. This is the only way that love can possibly begin to grow in our lives. Recognition that it is not there, and determination to do what is necessary to put it there—this is a beginning. Frankly, the kind of people who are hardest of all *for me* to love are the ones who smile with saccharine sweetness and say, "Oh, but I love everyone!" Just who are they fooling? If there is any reader who honestly thinks he does, I would like to meet that person, because I have been looking a long time for a first-class Christian saint! The tragedy, besides our families and friends, is that within the Christian family—in guilds and church groups, in coffee hours and vestries—there is often such an unashamed lack of Christian love. The first step is to recognize this truth and then try to do something about it.

The second step is equally simple, and without it there can be no increase in our spiritual temperature. It consists simply in ceasing to do the unkind thing to the other person. As long as one continues to let his animosity out on another in hostility or anger, there is no hope that love towards that person will increase. And yet, this is our perfectly natural reaction to wrong and injury. If one's wife complains about something, then one finds some soft spot in her life and complains right back. If a neighbor sweeps his leaves over into one's yard, one goes out and sweeps them right back. If someone hurts our feelings, we either try to return the hurt or else we turn our backs and quite pointedly give them the silent treatment.

Most of us are really quite civilized. We seldom go at each other with clubs or knives or fists—although I have heard of such things happening between husband and wife—but in the privacy of the home our least civilized side does show itself in more refined ways. Most of us, in fact, are very subtle in our cruelty, quite refined. And the second step is for us to realize that we are indulging in actions which can hardly be called loving, and bring them to a halt.

At the same time there is a corollary to this step which is most important. We must realize that we do get angry, that anger is one necessary function of the human being, the source of a part of our energy. Even anger which is misdirected cannot simply be repressed and forgotten without paying a deadly price. It is still there, working unconsciously and beyond our control, sometimes to make us hostile against others, sometimes attacking our bodies with tension and psychosomatic illness. We have to learn to deal with our anger, to face up to it if we are to work at being able to love.

There are several ways: one can examine it, write down just what is bothering him, sometimes talk it over with a friend and get his comfort and consolation. At times one may find an outer cause that needs to be changed, and go to work on it, or he may find there is nothing he can do on his own. One then finds, like Job, that he can cry out to God from the depth of his being and be heard, and that God is well able to bear the agony of man's anger and distress. And as I have found, once I have protested specifically to God about the things that are wrong, the next day is usually a happier time, especially for those close to me.

In other words, it is no sin to be angry. The sin is to nurse

anger in one's relationships, feeding it more and more griev-
ances without facing the actual causes squarely. For the nursed
anger becomes hate, and then love is defeated entirely. As Paul
wrote to the Ephesians, *"Even if you are angry, you must not
sin;* never let the sun set on your anger or else you will give the
devil a foothold" (4:26–27). It is up to us to keep bringing the
light and power of Christ to bear upon our anger.

In fact, this is the only way the next step is possible. This third
step is harder to accomplish, just because the tongue is such an
unruly member of the body. Not only must we stop doing unkind things to other people, we must stop saying unkind things
about them to any audience, no matter how receptive they are to
a juicy morsel. This takes real control. Only an extraordinary
circumstance will justify tearing down or criticizing any other
person. And in that case—if the other person is doing something
which really needs amendment—then the thing to do, of course,
is to go to that person and tell him with love, and only after one
has reflected deeply to see if the trouble is with them or with us.

This has not always been one of my rules of life. I remember
the exact place and time when I realized that I had no right to
speak critically or negatively about any other human being. I
was going with a friend to a wedding reception. She had been
studying Unity, and she remarked: "It showed me that I could
never again speak negatively or judgingly about other people."
This shook me. I suddenly realized that this had hardly been my
rule. I had particularly loved to pick out faults of other
clergy. . . . From that day on I have tried. I have often failed; but
then I try to get up again without too much remorse, and try
again. For I have come to realize that there can be no real
growth in love towards any specific person, or in love in general,
until one ceases talking negatively about that other person.
Doing unkindnesses and saying them wears ruts of evil in the
soul so that love cannot abide there.

The fourth step is simply to pray for those whom you find it
hard to love. This works in two different ways. In the first place,
it is very difficult to ask God to be really kind and generous and
take care of someone while we are trying to knock them down!

This makes one a first rate hypocrite. Nothing discourages the negative side of one's actions more than sincerely praying for the positive; one begins to change.

But this praying has another strange and mysterious effect; it has a metaphysical impact. I don't understand how or why, but it works. As one prays for the person who is disliked, there is a tendency for that person, too, to open up and change. I will never forget the experience of praying for a woman in one parish. I thought she was the most impossible and unpleasant person I knew. She was nasty, cantankerous, gossipy, and domineering. If prayer would help her, it would help anyone. And so I tried praying for her regularly. About the third week she called one day and wanted to come see me. In fear and trembling I made the appointment. But when she came, I was amazed. She told in a halting fashion that she just wanted me to know how much the church meant to her. She realized what a horrible person she was and knew how much worse she would have been without the effect of the church upon her life. . . . I realized that she suffered just as much being herself as I did being me, and we became good friends.

The fifth step is an interesting one. It consists of examining the life of the person whom we do not love (or like), and looking long enough to find something positive and creative in that person, something we can genuinely admire. *And you can find this in everyone.* With some people I'll admit it takes longer, but there is something good in everyone.

Then when the opportunity comes, you can simply say the good you have found rather than the evil. The effect of this is unbelievable. If you are in a group where the tongues are sharpened for moral dissection, just throw a positive tidbit into the conversation and the whole atmosphere changes. I remember hearing what happened in one group when the membership were taking their former president apart fault by fault. The list of her failings grew until someone quietly remarked, "But did you ever notice what a nice job she has done in raising her son." It was like a positive bombshell. The whole tone of the group changed, and the conversation about the woman dropped.

The last step is to do something kind for the person who has been hard for you to love. Think of something that will make that person happy, and then do it without their even knowing that you have done it. The effect is miraculous. One finds it very difficult to dislike the person whom he has made happy. It is almost inhuman to be able to. One can do either some little thing, or something bigger if it brings happiness. This inner kind of joy, of course, makes the other person more lovable too.

In the end it is usually *not* the people who do things for us whom we love, but the people for whom we do things. This is a fundamental psychological and spiritual law. It is one of the very reasons we love our children so much: We have done so much for them, just because we have had to, and because we have wanted to, and because they have needed us to do it. This works with those outside the family group as well as within it. If we will try it in both, we will find that our specific love will grow, and as it increases and develops, we will realize more and more fully the importance and power of love and the need for it.

Love is a reality, a power which appears to be anchored in the heart of human reality. As I have tried to suggest, it is central for Christian life. The task of the followers of Christ, it appears, is to love others as he loved us. This begins with ourselves and spreads outward towards our families and friends, through acquaintances, to the stranger and the enemy. Charles Williams once wrote that there were those things which need not be forgiven, those that ought to be forgiven, and those which could not be forgiven—and the Christian forgave them all. This might be paraphrased: There are those whom we want to love, those we don't care about loving, and those we can't love—and our Christian task is to try to love them all.

This is indeed a high calling. No wonder we need an eternity to work on it after we have done the best we can here on earth. We also need all the help right now that we can find. Each of us, on our own, can try the steps I have outlined, which are all ways of learning to love that have been tested in the experience of a number of people. In addition I have become convinced—also through a great deal of experience—that the educational process itself can be used in much the same way. Education itself can be developed into far more than a method of handing on information and ideas and beliefs. It can also be used as a way of stimulating individual growth, offering both teacher and student a wealth of ways of relating to themselves, to other human beings, and to God. Let us look now at education as a process of communicating these ways of relationship, these ways of prayer and love which are the essence of Christianity.

4

Education in Communication

Modern Christianity seldom stops to ask what unique value, what treasure it can offer the individual. Christian education these days seems to be aimed mostly at the acceptance of a package of ideas. What the individual does with these ideas is his own business. The person who is smart enough to learn from them and strong enough to lead a good Christian life will undoubtedly reap rewards. But this is as far as most of our current thinking about the personal value of Christian education goes. The individual ought to benefit, but we can hardly expect to gain anything which we could not earn by our own merit and moral effort in the course of ordinary living.

The idea of teaching ordinary Christians like you and me to seek power or direct action from God seems out of the question to most of us. We have learned that God operates by normal physical laws, and that only the most foolish souls believe that God can break through and change situations and even individual lives. We have learned the lessons of science and the virtues of faith, hope, and keeping a stiff upper lip almost too well. But our Christian theology has not taught us much about the personal values of prayer and of love. Our theology has become separated from our individual values and our ways of learning and communicating.

Christian thinking has come to ignore the task which gives theology its central, probably its only, reason for existing. This is the job of helping human beings come to know God, experience and relate to him, and then communicate this knowledge and these experiences to other people. This is a complex task, and in the long run there is no other task so important for our human welfare. Our whole valuation of ourselves and what we do depends almost entirely on how well we are able to relate to the central meaning or purpose in the universe. Just about the quickest way of losing energy and bringing one's life to a dead end is to conclude that there is no meaning to be found in human existence.

The job that theology faces is a difficult one, requiring a great deal of experience and knowledge and skill. It can probably be accomplished only as we Christians pool our talents and experience. As Christians realize their need to know the spiritual world and God, they will seek ways of communicating with these realities. For most of us the first hurdle is to break through our present hang-ups over the notion that only physical matter is real. As we have already discussed, there is good scientific evidence pointing to the existence of a spiritual world and to the reality of our contact with it. While facts like these will naturally lead certain individuals to a deep and productive interest in theology, most of us must find our way by means of direct experiences of one kind or another.

Most Christians need to find deeper experiences of the psyche or soul. They need to discover within themselves how God can communicate meaning and purpose to an individual, and how a person can then help others find similar experiences of their own. It is not all that easy, however, to persuade human beings to step out into new experiences, into unknown and untried territory. All kinds of fears—justified and unjustified, as well as the beliefs and illusions of a lifetime or longer—stand in the way. And this is just where Christian education comes into the picture. If this understanding of our need for central meaning in our lives is true, then we Christians have a great deal to learn about the ways in which such meaning is communicated and received, and this is a problem of Christian education.

In fact one can hardly imagine a problem closer to the heart of that education than this one of learning and teaching about the soul and how it can bring us into touch with the center of all meaning. Since in all its aspects this is a problem of communication, let us ask why modern Christianity is failing to communicate itself, and how education can be used to develop this kind of communication.

Towards a Theology of Communication

The difficulty for most Christian educators today comes from the fact that they cannot see outside of the current theology and its philosophy that dominate our present understanding of the world and everything that affects our lives. This thinking even determines how we communicate—or fail to do so—with ourselves and with other human beings. Since, in this world view, there seems to be no practical way of communicating with that center of reality which gives meaning to human life, Christian education for the most part simply ignores the growing evidence to the contrary. It fails to take this *experience* of human beings into consideration. Thus our education also ignores the strong evidence that in the long run we find value and meaning only in this way, and so it cannot prepare men and women for their total world, but educates them only for a portion of it.

Few theologians have realized that they need to understand the educational process. They have generally assumed that religion could be communicated as a set of intellectual truths which anyone with a bright enough mind could take in and assimilate. History does not exactly support this assumption, and neither do the recent surveys of religion by social scientists, as James Michael Lee has amply documented in his several books. What these recent studies do suggest is that very likely we need to go beyond any philosophical approach to education and develop a theology of communication.

In the late reflections of one important theologian there is at least a beginning, and a thoughtful one. Paul Tillich, in his *Theology of Culture,* included a chapter on "A Theology of Education." His concluding observations were addressed as a question to Christian ministers and teachers about "Communicating the Christian Message."

Tillich discussed the three major aims of education, pointing out the loss to the culture when they become separated from man's basic search for meaning. He showed how *technical* education, which provides the know-how to deal with the outer world, has moved in on the *humanistic* and *inducting* goals, almost eliminating these two aims. What passes for humanistic education today no longer seeks to develop the individual's potential, but mainly deals with forms from the past. Inducting or initiatory education—aimed at giving the individual participation in the social group and its values—is used by religious groups in a limited way. But these values are quickly lost when the adult moves into the ordinary world where inducting education is the effective servant of an industrial and technical society.

The church, as Tillich saw, must continue to introduce the growing human being to the mythical language and the power of Christian symbols. At the same time it must try to help him go beyond this induction and question it. Certainly Tillich was right in this. The collective culture, the culture which is primarily nonindividual, uses inducting education to perpetuate itself, often at the expense of the individual. Individual development comes as the ideas of the collective, whether primitive or modern, are challenged.

These ideas open up a fresh perspective on Christian education, while the understanding of the world which we are considering requires a further step. The understanding of central purpose in all that we do requires that we look at education overall, at *what* we are communicating, with *whom* we are communicating, and *how* we are communicating. In each step we will find that we are communicating not only with teacher or students, but also with ourselves and with God. We will find all kinds of ways, things that can be done to bring this central meaning into our own lives and thus the lives of other people. This is one meaning of a theology of communication. First of all, this understanding of Christian education starts with a much broader idea of what is to be taught.

It sees inducting education as a stage in the development of every individual. Induction into the culture in which one is born is necessary, just as the child must learn to identify with his own family, but either identification is still preliminary to self-consciousness. Where the individual is seen as having a unique relationship with the spiritual world, a unique destiny and value, education does not end with this stage. Anything that is encountered through this initiatory education may be reexamined and tested by the individual to see if it fits his experience. This is the very point at which our young people seem to be today. They are no longer satisfied with being taken into the culture, like joining a fraternity.

Indeed the culture itself, to stay alive, must continue on beyond this stage. The great Catholic council in 1965, Vatican II, recognized this and came out with an emphasis on the individual which represents both the spirit of the times and the spirit of Jesus of Nazareth. Just as it took almost two thousand years to realize that slavery did not belong among Christians, so it has taken very nearly the same time to understand that conscious, growing human beings need their own encounters with God, and that religion cannot be just induced and stabilized in them. If the institutional church does not wake up to this fact, it is in for even worse days than it has had. Either the church must explore the experiential base which can be available to people, and then educate them to know and to build on it, or they will look elsewhere for these basic experiences.

A far broader technical education is also needed than the present training in the sciences, arts, and engineering, which deal with only half of the reality to which man is exposed. As Jung remarked in his interview with John Freeman on the BBC film *Face to Face with Dr. Jung*, the problems that are most difficult for people do not come from these areas, but rather from our lack of understanding of ourselves and the nonphysical world that surrounds us. Practical technical education is needed to provide the skills to deal with our psyches or souls and with this other world which we encounter through them.

In the first place, we need to learn how we can resist psychic or spiritual infections, much as we need medical techniques to fight bacterial infections. And then, because this realm of experience is known only through the psyche, understanding of the psyche is essential so that we can see and understand our experience as clearly as possible. Skills are needed to avoid distortion in psychic perception and understanding, just as refined scientific methods are developed to avoid the distortions in ordinary seeing and hearing. It is more difficult, of course, to do this in dealing with the world of experience that comes through direct contact with the psyche, but this is possible and it is certainly needed. In fact, this is one of the major tasks of religion, as well as of psychology.

The base of humanistic education is greatly widened in our framework. Coming to know the spiritual world and the psyche that must receive it requires the greatest development of a person's capacities. One may have the greatest insights from this "inner" spiritual world and still not be able to distinguish what has value from that which comes from destructive spiritual influences, or from wish-fulfillment and pride. And unless one can bring the insights to bear on his own life and life around him, they might as well be bubbles on a stream. To do this one has his own personality, and what speaks through it, to work with. He has to depend upon his experiences and values, his ability to work with others, comparing and then feeling his way among these experiences. We are explorers in this world of spirit; we are like physicists looking into the atom with no microscope or tracking device except their own personalities.

The task within this framework, then, is to transmit the meanings and symbols of Christianity as best we can while we learn new ways of approaching their source, and at the same time try to grow enough as human beings to handle the new ways of experience and what they bring. This is a big order. In fact it is far too big for men to consider if they are thinking about doing it on their own.

But that is just the point we are making. The church says that it believes in God. What we have suggested is that, if the church is willing to test this proposition in experience, it will find that God is more than just an Aristotelian category of the known world. Men will find a source of meaning and power beyond their own, power that is not just an untapped residue of their own abilities. But this cannot be communicated by any stretch of the imagination to people who also confine man to a particular slot in the easily known and predictable world. These people, who are probably in the majority inside the church as well as out of it, hold a theory of personality that keeps large areas of experience at arm's length, or farther. Before communication can begin, one has to recognize this barrier and start the job of penetrating it.

A Common Theory of Personality

Most of the people who hold this popular theory of personality would be quite upset at the suggestion that they have a psychological point of view. They consider it simply a matter of dealing with facts, and they are extremely suspicious of psychology; it might as well be a four-letter word for many. Nonetheless, these people do express a psychology, which they hold without giving it much thought. And the trouble with holding a view without reflecting on it is that the view generally controls the individual rather than the other way around. When ideas are simply assumed, they cannot be criticized or examined because one does not know that he has them; instead, one thinks they are "facts." Thus, when something seems as obvious as this idea about human beings, it is time to start doubting and questioning it.

According to this view, human personality has quite a simple and easily understood structure, mostly built out of conscious exposure to things and ideas. Since man comes into the world as a blank page on which life chalks up its traces, society has two responsibilities towards him. Its job first is to direct the experiences of the growing human being so as to turn out a society of adults filled with the right content, and then to back this up with some system of reward and punishment. This psychology is backed up by a theory of education which follows right in line, including all the sources.

The role of the educator is to feed the right mixture of appropriate experiences into human beings, much as one would feed data into a very sensitive computer. His responsibility (once this role is defined) is to select and shape the patterns of the developing person in accordance with the social pattern, or the educator's pattern, or some other standard. B. F. Skinner is explicit about the way this theory has been expected to work in practice; apply the correct "operant conditioning" and one will get the desired results. Basically Skinner considers the human being about as complex as a pigeon. In fact, this thinking—which has been around quite a while, although not as clearly stated as Skinner puts it—is very idealistic about being able to shape individuals in the most desirable way. If the input is correct, they will become acceptable, productive, law-abiding members of the group.

But if a person does not turn out this way, it is the result of either the wrong input or a perverse will. One must try to correct the conditioning, but if the individual resists and refuses to take on the correction rationally, it is concluded that his will needs to be altered. In this case the second task of society comes into play. It has the responsibility of meting out certain rewards, but more especially of punishing, to produce the proper conditioning and alter the will. Individuals whose actions show that they do not have the right ideas or habits, whose will is simply perverse, must be brought into line. And if punishment fails to change a man towards a more socially acceptable pattern of behavior, then the only alternative is to banish him from the social group so that his presence will not act as the rotten apple in the barrel.

Obviously I have used a fairly heavy hand to picture these ideas. Still, this does not exaggerate the way most of our law courts, most mental institutions and prisons, and many of our schools and families have operated. Mental institutions that were run on this theory left most of their patients without hope of recovery, and most prisoners treated in this way end up back in prison, confirmed in their antisocial attitudes. As for families, the people who have come to me in real need of counseling have almost invariably come from family situations in which the basis of relationship was essentially the theory of personality I have described. Nor have churches been exactly free of this understanding and its effect on the way church people treat each other and their clergy. There have been religious schools that followed it to the letter, even to regulating the width of the strap in the principal's office!

The trouble is that the church, by a strange alchemy, has managed to ignore the difference between this thinking and the understanding of Jesus and his followers. The church is out of touch with its own reality, and it does not even see that thinkers in other fields have been forced by various parts of reality to take a new look at the world and man. The church has not realized the depth and complexity of human beings and the kind of world that touches them. Until it is willing to take the risk of breaking out of our common thinking about ourselves—people's essentially Aristotelian and materialistic view of human beings—it cannot see the depth of reality, let alone communicate this to the depth of any individual.

The gospel was originally spread by men who were willing to take this risk, who had no social power to depend on. Jesus and most of the leaders of the early church were outlaws from the social group, and the main reason Christianity made the imprint it did was that it had a following who cared for and were interested in one another, and because they experienced breakthroughs of power that astounded the ancient world. Paul made this very explicit in his important letter to the Romans when he summed up:

> For I will not venture to speak of anything except what Christ has wrought through me to win obedience from the Gentiles, by word and deed, by the power of signs and wonders, by the power of the Holy Spirit . . . (Romans 15:18–19 RSV).

As the French philosopher Festugière has remarked, Christians had a sense of being "members of one another. . . ." If it had not been there, "the world would still be pagan. And the day when it is no longer there, the world will be pagan once again."

When communicating the Christian gospel is understood in this way, it has an exciting quality which is quite lacking when learning about Christianity is reduced to transmitting a set of propositions, or final, logical ideas. This is not only dull (no matter how satisfying it may be to the teacher), but it is seldom effective in changing people's lives and behavior. As James Michael Lee has shown repeatedly, little relation can be found between the individual's ethical and religious behavior (or practice) and what he has studied about religion and ethics. Such teaching may be very close to demonic, in fact, if one feels obliged to force-feed another person, who may or may not be ready for it.

Even more important, this method actually discourages learning through experience about the spiritual reality that is basic to Christianity. Quite recently a group of students in a private school realized this and tried to do something about it. They approached the woman who, interestingly enough, teaches both physics and religion in the school, and asked her why they couldn't get into religion the same way they did physics. She was fascinated by the idea of helping these high school seniors search for answers, and together they started questioning and experimenting. The church, however, has been less certain of its ground than this teacher and her students, and they found few approaches to experiences with which the group could experiment.

Many people take a nostalgic view of the way religion and culture are handed on from one generation to another within a collective social group. Primitive or collective society does, of course, transmit its culture, but usually with fear and without much regard for individual value or worth; this is the point Henri Bergson makes in *The Two Sources of Morality and Religion.* Any variation from the norm is suspect and may be suppressed by the collective group. Christianity, on the other hand, speaks of our essential value as individuals, our almost infinite depth and complexity, and of our ability to make our own contact with the realm of spirit. An understanding quite beyond the collective pattern must be transmitted if this religion of ours is to be consistent with its own genius. Where then does one start to make this effective?

Where To Begin

Probably the best way to start today is with small groups of adults, actually study groups or classes, in which a close and caring relationship can be developed, and in which the realities we have been discussing can be talked about, but not talked to death. This takes skillful leadership because it involves the individual's acceptance of both himself and others. Only in such an atmosphere is it possible for these realities of spirit to be encountered and (to some extent) shared. It is necessary to get below the surface of the individual personality, but this is a process of discovering and accepting the realities of one's own being, not a cleaning out job like an encounter group. For this reason it takes a leader who knows and accepts himself quite thoroughly, and also grasps quite clearly the relation of psychological understanding to religious realities.

This relationship which can mesh an encounter with the realm of spirit can also be found through individual counseling where a minister or others have the desire and have had sufficient experience in this area themselves. Individuals can also be started on this way through groups who seek to meditate and pray openly together; this also requires strong leadership if it is to avoid either flying off on individual tangents or becoming bogged down in just ideas about religion.

The liturgy of the church, of course, can offer an individual the deepest and fullest encounter with spiritual realities once one has started on this way. In the central act of communion, as we are able to bring more and more of ourselves to the altar, we can find this encounter through the living presence of Christ who cares and accepts beyond all others.

Individuals who are growing, and thus are better able to approach the realities of spirit on their own, find that they can often minister to someone else when there is need. But the small class group undoubtedly remains the best way of introducing people to this view of the world, and of exploring new material with those who wish to continue growing and building new relationships.

This requires, however, a more adult approach to Christianity than we have been accustomed to. Religion has to be seen as more than moral law or a collective pattern that can be instilled into children once and for all. There are also difficulties about getting support for such a program. When the proposal for study groups was first made to the official lay board of my own church, there was more hostility than I encountered at any other time during the twenty years I was rector there, including even the time when there was an outbreak of tongue speaking. The board did not want to spend the money to pay a competent professional educatior, whose value was soon proved, both in the adult groups and also in preparing an imaginative program for children.

Why is it so likely, then, that acceptance of oneself and real concern for the other person will convey a more Christian view of the world than the best-intentioned criticism or the effort to eliminate or avoid anything unpleasant in either person? And more especially, why is effort needed on experience for adults, instead of children? Let us consider first the needs of the growing child, and second of the adult, by picturing two individuals standing in relation to the physical and the spiritual worlds, much as I have diagrammed this whole relation in discussing prayer on p. 30.

Let us imagine that they are facing each other in our space-time world, and that one of them is a teacher and the other a child. They have come together, Robinson Crusoe-like, on this island in space, each bringing his own complex personality structure. The adult's is more complex at the tip—there are conscious attitudes and personal memories that have been filed away and forgotten. But each has his own early conditioning, his tendencies or type structure (probably partly inherited), his own depth of unconscious, and the child is generally more open to the realities of the spiritual world that surrounds them both.

In the Christian view we propose, the goal of the teacher—or parent or other adult—is to help the child grow so that he will become able to deal with both the outer physical world and the spiritual one that bears directly in on him. In the beginning the task is to turn the child's attention towards the outer world, helping him learn how to deal with the physical world and to separate these experiences from ones of the spiritual world. But this does not mean suppressing the latter kind of experiences, for one's hope is that, when the child has matured, he will come to a relationship with the creative center of the spiritual world.

But, first of all, the child needs to develop a strong center of his personality. In psychological language, he needs a well-developed ego (not in the negative sense that many religionists use this term). A strong ego, which is necessary in the outer world, is even more indispensable if the person is to encounter the spiritual world with any degree of safety. And how can something be offered to God that the person has never had? If the goal in the end is to give up one's life in order to gain it, then the beginning must be to have a life to give up.

As the child grows, his orientation must still be towards the outer world, building a base for his life like a pyramid, step by step. His curiosity and learning, his need for friends, for sexual identification, finally for love and the work he must fulfill, all radiate outwards. At the same time, the maturity that he achieves in each of these steps depends largely on the ability of the adult opposite him, the teacher, to provide a climate of warmth and empathy. The child and young person need rules and structure to grow. The adult requires maturity and a source of inner strength to present the rules and structure so that they neither confine the growth nor warp it by too much freedom.

For the time being the young person is given his understanding of the realities of religion through story and image, symbols and myths. Then the time comes when he wishes to stand apart and test what he has learned for himself. And at this point the child changes. He still needs the support of the adult who is secure in his knowledge and maturity. But from this time on a person's experience can pose questions at any time, forcing him to look inward and ask what is happening to him. This is the point that so many of our young people have reached today. It is the point at which maturity can begin, and also the point at which a person can choose his own way religiously. At this critical stage the adult who is secure himself will encourage separation and independence and testing, for each individual must make his own relationship with both the outer and inner worlds of experience.

When one does turn inward, even briefly, he usually finds destructive, annihilating aspects of spiritual reality, which are more than he can handle. His need then is for the creative spirit which is characterized by love. If he has had an accepting relationship, one of warmth and understanding and freedom, it will be easier for him to turn then for guidance. At this point the goal of the mature adult is to give him support and assurance so that he can find his own way among these realities and develop a life style characterized by mature caring for others. This is very difficult for any adult to communicate unless one has known such relationship and can exemplify these qualities himself. Can the blind lead the blind?

Such a goal is almost unknown in our culture today. Instead, almost universally, human beings are only partially accepted. Qualities of personality that are "bad," that are blamed for people's troubles, are rejected; the effort is to eliminate them. Some churches are committed to helping people look within themselves for this reason. But the basis is the antiquated theory of personality that we have discussed. The purpose is to find what is wrong in the person and get rid of it so that he can get back into operation like other normal people.

There are two results. First, one finds anger and hostility simmering within people. It often comes out in the privacy of home, and it is also seen in groups mediated for the purpose of encountering and learning something about the anger. Without a mediator who is well aware of his own hostility and quick to step in with ways of handling what comes, the net result is simply to compound the effect of these destructive forces, leaving most people worse off than ever. All of us have a natural tendency to anger and hostility. To be quite honest and genuine, we sometimes have to let it out. The person who thinks that he has none of this in himself does not know himself very well. Mature individuals know their own hostility; while they may not always succeed, they at least try to use it to serve a creative purpose (by our definition, a purpose of loving concern).

As I have tried to show clearly in my study of Christian meditation, *The Other Side of Silence*, this is one of the real reasons for education in the kind of prayer we have discussed. This way of allowing images to arise in prayer can open up the hidden unconscious angers that seethe below the surface in most of us. Even more important, we can then learn to let the image of the risen Christ enter into these times of prayer and redirect our anger and hostility into more creative channels, so that these destructive forces are not turned loose either within or on the outside world.

The second result of rejecting parts of the personality is to wipe out one of the most central purposes of religion in the Christian tradition. So long as being "normal" means avoiding whole areas of experience that can play into the psyche, there is no possibility of working toward wholeness or integration of the personality, toward that health of body, mind and soul which Jesus stressed throughout his ministry. Yet this goal itself, if intelligibly expressed, communicates the Christian spirit to men better than most of the things that fill books about God in the abstract.

For this reason, and also because so much of the young person's religious understanding is shaped by the parents, we have given first priority to groups of parents who will try realistically to accept a wider range of human experience and more of their own personalities. Indeed, so much of the child's ideas and values are formed in the home that it is even suggested in the Catholic church that the parish grade school is not the best way to communicate religion. In order to begin to reach children, the communication of religion will necessarily be focused upon young adults and the younger parents.

This is also the most open field for religion to take hold. From high school age on, most young people are trying to find their own identity; they are separating from family values and practices. It is not that they are irreligious, but rather that they are seeking the individual relation we have discussed. If they are inhibited from going their own way, they often turn irrevocably against the framework they have known. But if the church can offer experience and real relationship to these young people, particularly to those in revolt against the materialism of their parents and seeking experience in drugs, meditation, or the occult, they will be able to find the inner journey and its outer counterpart of a loving life style. At the same time, their parents, puzzled and bewildered, are almost equally ready for experience and acceptance. What, then, are the most important things for a group to consider who will try to communicate this?

A Basis for Communicating Christianity

First of all we need a climate in which communication can be open. Whatever materials are dealt with, the process is one of experiencing together. This is possible only where mature Christian love is the climate so that the individual is opened up. This reality, the *agape* described by Paul in 1 Corinthians 13—which we have considered from a practical standpoint—can then touch each life. Communication in this sense is more than ordinary human relationship in words and thoughts. Rather, it is communication in depth, of spirit with spirit, in which one does not so much take action as allow the Spirit that is characterized by love to act through him. When Christians are effective in this way, their human love is used sacramentally, much as the bread and wine are used by the same Spirit in the Communion.

Process and content cannot be separated, however. The whole is like a three-legged stool that collapses if one leg is removed. All three legs—human beings and their ability to react, content or materials and an intellectual framework in which their meaning can be grasped, and the Spirit that enlivens both—are equally essential. But it is not an easy job to get these three into the reactor at once; this requires the best we have to give, emotionally, intellectually, and devotionally.

1. There must first be an understanding of the world which intelligent people can accept, a framework in which the materials are no longer untouchable theological ideas or actions, as

most seminaries present them. For this reason it is often the hardest for us clergy to understand experiential Christianity; yet theological materials (including the understanding of reality we are discussing) are only a skeleton until human beings are willing to experiment with them and see what happens. And this requires a view of the world from which people can see the outcome as potentially meaningful. Thus some model or framework representing the world as accurately as possible is essential if people are to see that there is something meaningful in their ordinary, daily lives which is beyond the space-time-material experience of the individual. We shall consider such a model of reality more fully in the final chapter.

Along with this understanding, there is a need to consider how we use language to convey meaning. The rules of language that all of us have absorbed definitely favor limited communication about objects in the physical world. Perhaps our words have had to originate in this way. But when the rules for using them also make it easier to speak of one tangible thing at a time, then it means thinking carefully if we wish to discuss relations between things, or speak of something that is not sensory to begin with. One of the most interesting and liberating subjects to consider is an understanding of how words can work for us instead of helping to make us slaves of our ideas.

Much of this understanding is offered by the general semantics movement in this country. It is available for general use in a simplified, outline form in *General Semantics: An Outline Survey* by Kenneth G. Johnson. Applied to religion, this material gives a start on more open communication.

2. Understanding ourselves and how our lives are directed comes next on the specific list. And this means opening up a new possibility for anyone who looks deeply within himself. One may well find that his or her life is guided far more by a deep search for religious meaning and for wholeness of personality than by the outer circumstances that usually seem so significant and determining.

This is one of Jung's most basic ideas, and his *Modern Man in Search of a Soul* offers one of the best introductions to this understanding of ourselves. This should be followed by John A. Sanford's *The Kingdom Within*, which develops this view by considering the meaning of the sayings of Jesus. *Creation Continues* by Fritz Kunkel gives another treatment of this whole idea, while Jung's *Two Essays on Analytical Psychology*, his *Memories, Dreams, Reflections*, and *Man and His Symbols*, and later *The Way of All Women* by Esther Harding, offer additional material to build on.

3. A third essential approach is to dreams, even though this apparently means breaking new ground to get back to the Christian understanding of them. There are certainly enough dreams in the Bible to suggest their importance. But the idea that these experiences need further understanding, as the fathers of the church considered, has not received much attention in our time.

Specifically, dreams form a bridge between the need to know ourselves and the need to know the reality, the power and direction of the Holy Spirit. With the help of dreams, the results of an encounter with God can be observed. And it is just such observable results which give meaning to the Christian framework and the effort of working towards wholeness of personality; they are basic to the communication of Christianity.

My own book, *Dreams: The Dark Speech of the Spirit*, deals with this approach, both in the Christian tradition and in the thinking of Jung, and it offers an introduction to the subject. Another valuable sourcebook is *Dreams: God's Forgotten Language*, in which John Sanford has applied a similar understanding to a group of modern dreams which brought new life and new conviction to the individuals. *The Meaning in Dreams and Dreaming* by Maria F. Mahoney, which offers a clear summary of Jung's understanding of dreams, might be a valuable follow-up.

4. The whole area of prayer and meditation, including prayer for healing, also needs to be considered. While meditative prayer must take place alone and in silence, it is also possible among groups of people who make the effort to enter a state of utter silence together. The individuals can then wait for images to arise from their own inner depths, or a leader experienced in

this practice can share a directed meditation. In either case, images will usually come spontaneously to at least some of the group. For nearly twenty years I met once a week with such a prayer group in the church of which I was rector. Most of the time we found that the joint effort to meditate helped each individual reach this state. With leaders trained in psychological as well as religious understanding, groups can experiment with this way of learning about ourselves and some of the deeper ways in which we can discover and relate to the central meaning in our world.

There is also a great deal that we need to learn about the whole process of meditation as it relates to the Christian point of view and about various practices that can help people reach a meditative state. My book *The Other Side of Silence: A Guide to Christian Meditation* attempts to deal with this subject as fully as possible. It is the only study in modern times which tries to open up the traditional meaning of meditation for Christians, and uses the insights of psychology and of other religious practices to help them learn this practice. It also points up the relation of Christian meditation to dreams and certain other Christian experiences.

In churches where prayer and laying-on-of-hands for healing is accepted as valuable, this direct scramental approach can be a powerful way of communicating the Christian spirit. There is no question that healings do occur now and then, much as they are described in the New Testament, and these experiences are certainly convincing. Those occurring among teen-age drug users through conversion experiences are one example. But this is not the only aspect that needs to be stressed. For instance, physical healing may be related to the person's wholeness, either as a prelude or as the result of his growth and integration. There are also times when healing occurs, particularly medical healing, whose value is only partly realized because the person lacks any central meaning in his life.

Much can be learned about the central meaning of Christianity by considering carefully the healing actions of Jesus described throughout the gospels. Both psychology and psychosomatic medicine also offer valuable insights; much of this material is found in *Persuasion and Healing*, a careful study by Jerome Frank of Johns Hopkins which clearly suggests the reality of Christian healing. The book I have written on *Healing and Christianity* also summarizes this material, as well as the history of healing in the church, and suggests the place of healing in the Christian world view which I propose. Agnes Sanford's *The Healing Light and Behold Your God* offer an invaluable approach to the actual experience and practice of healing.

As individuals come to appreciate the reality of the spiritual world, there are various areas of religious practice, certain spiritual disciplines, and the whole charismatic movement that groups may want to explore, as well as areas of psychology, philosophy, and history. In fact, when this program was first tried, within five years hundreds of adults were coming for college level seminars, and they took home far more than book learning. The results were seen in family after family, and young people came to find out about this church which even tried to understand the ancient *I Ching;* many of them stayed to become members.

5. In addition, for two reasons leaders and individuals alike will want to understand the variations and dynamics of personality structure as fully as they can. Knowledge of our own personality structure and how we generally function is one way of learning about ourselves. And if Christians are concerned to accept and express loving care for others, then it is necessary to begin to know the other person. There is not much chance of knowing another person as long as one can pick out only the similarities to oneself. Jung's understanding of personality types and differences in personality structure makes it possible to know and appreciate individual differences. This is so important for Christian education that we shall consider it in a separate section. As we shall see, it opens up real possibilities of a theology of communication.

Religion and Personality Type

We shall look briefly at this understanding of personality structure because several students have written about it fully and in a clear and interesting way. Probably the best study to start with is *Introduction to Type* by Isabel Briggs Myers, which gives a clear description of the theory and method of type testing. Her *Manual: The Myers-Briggs Type Indicator* puts together the results of several years of testing and verification. Jung developed the theory in depth in *Psychological Types*, showing something of how he arrived at it, and in *Lectures on Jung's Typology*, Marie-Louise von Franz and James Hillman present a wealth of detail about individuals in relation to their type structures. P. W. Martin also discusses the theory in *Experiment in Depth*. In addition, the Myers-Briggs Type Indicator Test is readily available and easy to administer and score; with the help of Mrs. Myers' *Introduction to Type*, individuals can learn a great deal about personality type through understanding their own structures.

Jung was interested in how people function in the world. Starting from his original descriptions of *introversion* and *extraversion* (which have since become household words), he came to see that people also differ greatly in how they prefer to deal with their experiences. Some people are *judging* in attitude and prefer to look a situation over and come to a decision about it (and if extraverted, they will probably act; or if introverted, they generally try to get someone else to take action). There are others who would rather not reach a decision, because they would rather look for more facts and continue to consider all the possibilities; these people are basically *perceptive* in orientation.

In addition each of these groups is further split four ways by the way they function in judging or perceiving. There is a *thinking* type who reaches decisions (or nondecisions) on the basis of logic and studying what is reasonable; the opposite is the *feeling* type, the person who considers the human values involved in a situation and arrives at a value judgment (or perception) which is a structured way of looking at reality. Or again, a person (either judging or perceptive in attitude) may function mainly through either sensation or intuition. The *sensation* type gathers his impressions through the physical senses, the *intuitive* through an inner "sixth" sense, and thinking or feeling then develops as a subsidiary function. Similarly, the thinking and feeling types generally develop one of the other two—sensation or intuition—as an auxiliary. With sixteen basic combinations, the shades of difference are almost infinite.

This means that each person develops a definite strength in dealing with the world, and also a very definite weakness. The person whose strength lies in thinking is often completely unaware of human values and is utterly amazed if he finds that someone has been hurt by his logically reasoned action. A person who has developed mainly his sensation function may belittle the idea of finding something out intuitively. Certain strengths, in fact, come to dominate a culture, simply because they are valued above others by that culture.

In the introverted culture of medieval times, for instance, the introverted intuitive and feeling types were encouraged, while today the value is put on extraversion, thinking and sensation which are needed to make good business executives. The person who does not develop these strengths is left with a sore spot around the unconscious, weak function. The introverted, intuitive person knows he cannot do the things that are valued by society, and even the church. He is often a failure before he starts. Yet no one type is superior to another; they are all needed. The person who is accepted and sees value in his dominant function can rely on other people and their strengths. One can even take the time that is needed to bring his weaker side—which is unconscious and often highly creative—into play.

Religion in particular needs all the various functions. But so often religion has been presented for only one type. When religion becomes only doctrine, a set of propositions that have to be accepted intellectually, it has little relevance or interest for the person who is interested in human values, the feeling type. When quiet and inner devotion are presented as all that matter, those who are extraverted and sensation-oriented are not touched where they are. Or if only a need for social action is offered, the intuitive and the thinking types are lost and their interest slips away.

Instead, if religion is understood as having the central purpose of discovering how human beings can bridge a relation between God and the immediate world, then approaches of all kinds are needed. The only way that man can come to know the central meaning of the universe in any degree is to experience this power from all sides. God cannot be pinned down to a single description, and individuals of every type are needed to find approaches. Then communication between God and man becomes possible, and communication between men on every level becomes essential. Every man, just because of his difference in personality structure, becomes important as a possible avenue to God. Basically this is the meaning of a theology of communication. The New Testament expression of this is seen in the description of the church as the "body of Christ"—a unified organism which is able to accommodate incredible diversity—indeed, *depends upon* the diversity for its very existence.

Thus, it is essential for us to realize that we each have our own individual way of reacting to the world, our own way of relating which is different from others. Once we recognize this, we will not try unconsciously (or consciously) to force others into our mold. Instead we will work towards relating to and communicating with them. There is a place for each of us, for the religious thinker, the religious activist, the expert in the devotional life, and the religious artist or builder. There are many different ways of experiencing and living the religious life, each with its difficulties and its values and rewards.

The task of the religious educator is to help each person find his own type, his own way, and to help him relate to the weaker, less conscious side from which new value can come. As Marie-Louise von Franz has remarked, one's weaker, less conscious function is like a valuable horse that cannot be whipped or trained to take the bit and saddle. With patience, one can get close enough to whisper in his ear, and even ride him without being thrown at the wrong time. But this is a complex, time-consuming business. As the way to wholeness of the personality, the way to relate to the unconscious where the spiritual realm can be found, it is also the business of religion, which itself is complex and time-consuming. But there is help in some of the newer educational thinking. Let us look at religious education, or the communication of religion to both child and adult, from this newer point of view.

Implementing Education of the Whole Man

There are a number of recent studies of the educational process that are valuable for teachers and leaders who want to communicate religion as we are suggesting. In the first place, Dr. Jung has sketched out some of the implications of his point of view for education. His educational ideas are found in *Development of Personality,* volume seventeen of his collected works. Frances Wickes has also written deeply and well from the same point of view; in *The Inner World of Childhood* she describes the child's development in relation to the world of autonomous or spiritual realities found in the unconscious.

Jung, however, was more concerned with the psychological inferences that could be drawn from his view. He seldom stepped into religious territory to suggest what should or should not be done, but left it to the church and those concerned with religion to put his ideas to work. As we have tried to indicate, his psychological point of view has a clearly religious side, although its implications have not been worked out for religious education.

Perhaps the most important understanding for us to grasp from Jung's thinking to begin with is the complexity of man and the world around him—both physical and spiritual—and the rejection of any simple or easy educational method. And second is the importance of our job, which seems to increase its difficulty. Even the most elementary communication is difficult, while communication about the deepest experiences of the spirit, which are a part of our world of experience, are the most difficult and by far the most important of all.

Since the point of view we have developed is essentially empirical in the broadest sense, the religious educator who is trying out this standpoint will want the best empirical data available.

Indeed, we will welcome such data as an addition to our understanding of human beings and the world in which they interact. Studies like Ronald T. Hyman's *Teaching: Vantage Points for Study* will help to direct and support our efforts in religious education. Studies like these show us that fear usually inhibits learning, while a warm and accepting environment generally stimulates the learning process. We will also learn ways of checking ourselves and other educators to see whether we are communicating at all.

From Carl Rogers' *Freedom to Learn* one also realizes that an open group with genuineness and freedom of decision as well as warmth and empathy, often enables individuals to develop their own abilities far more rapidly. Rogers supports this point with data from the social sciences, as well as providing the theory and specific classroom instances. The behavioral and experimental studies of both animals and men have also produced findings which have implications for teaching and learning. The religious educator will want to know not only the results of Piaget's research, but also the religious conclusions and other inferences which Ronald Goldman has drawn from them and tested.

Unfortunately Christian education has incompletes to make up in communication and educational skills and data, and it cannot make them up by continuing to cut classes, avoiding experience. As James Michael Lee points out so clearly in *The Shape of Religious Instruction,* the net result has been reliance on prejudice and logical theology rather than on a working knowledge, and this has not produced effective religious education. How then can we start to make up for lost time?

Teaching the Class in Religion

First of all, leading or teaching an actual class in religion is not easy, and it cannot be done en masse. It is seldom possible to communicate this kind of religious approach so that it takes hold in a group of more than twelve or fifteen people. Early Christianity realized this and took time to prepare new converts. First let us compare the dynamics of this slower, more complex way of communicating religion with the ordinary ways we have known of teaching religion, illustrating the various possibilities by means of a diagram.

We have the teacher, T, and the group members, A, B, and C. Each individual consists of both his conscious and unconscious (T', A', B', C') personalities. Each one has his own individual history, type structure, complexes, fears, desires, which appear only to a limited extent in his conscious, verbalized behavior.

If teachers use what has been called the "transmission theory" of education—the idea so common among religious educators today of religious proclamation—they will structure the class situation entirely towards a conscious relationship. They will try to bring each of the conscious, rational wills to accept certain ideas about theology and morals. Each individual will then "integrate" this doctrinal system. And some teachers may well bring all the conscious personalities to perfect agreement. But the problem with this idea (besides the arrogance of assuming so much certitude) is that the moment A', B', and C', begin to exert an influence, the learning that has reached only into the conscious mind is quickly pushed aside; it has little further effect.

On the other hand, with a moralistic approach the teacher

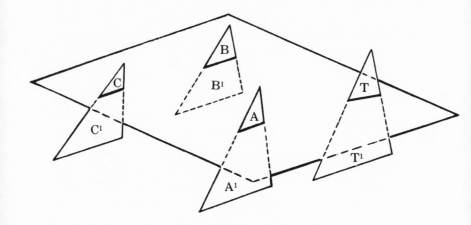

tries to shape a *total* response by each individual. By attempting to influence behavior more than the intelligence, one tries to bring all the individuals to respond in one specific way to the religious object. For instance, in the Catholic instruction modeled on the early ideas of the Society of St. Sulpice, every effort is made to shape the individual towards a certain pattern of "holiness." The use of devotions, the commitment to certain religious acts and practices, all the trappings of a particular religious way, all are an effort to influence A', B', and C'.

Unfortunately, the dependency needs of the teacher often force the student (particularly at certain suggestible times) to an acceptance of the pattern which still belongs only to the teacher. When the student begins to use his own individual consciousness, if he has understood the emphasis of Jesus on individuality, he is very likely to throw the baby out with the bath water. Once he feels tied down by the pattern, and realizes that this doesn't sound much like Christ, the whole enterprise is often rejected.

Or again, once in a while a very skillful and capable teacher comes along who is able to reach and shape both the conscious and the unconscious attitudes in his students. But when he does this, shaping them to his own model, he cuts the individuals off from following their own direction, and real harm may be done. If the individual realizes what has been done, a reaction usually takes place; or if the student remains unconscious, the results may be tension, with various ways of suffering or projecting it.

Our present knowledge of the human psyche and of the total world, particularly as we have outlined it, suggests a different approach. As I see it, the immediate task of religious education is to provide the conditions in which the following objectives can be realized.

1. The individual ego—the rational, conscious will—will be allowed to emerge in the strength of its own individuality. This means self-acceptance born of being accepted, and it is true of adults as well as children. Some adults still have ordinary maturing to achieve.

2. These developing personalities can then, within the group

process, come to a natural encounter with the totality of others. In this way one learns about his own depth, as well as the depth of others, and the longing of the individual for his own wholeness may then be allowed to emerge. This is possible only if both teacher and students alike are involved in an honest encounter with each other as individuals, encountering negative elements as well as positive. This is to be understood as an important part of the religious process. If we take Jesus of Nazareth seriously, the wholeness of the person is one religious goal in itself, and this first step is an essential preparation for a later, more specifically religious encounter.

The reason Jesus spoke such harsh words about the Pharisees and the reason he reproached men who judge others, was the same. By acting in this way they avoided any encounter with the depth of *themselves.* Self-knowledge would have changed their behavior; it is a necessity before much growth in the religious way is possible. The group encounter can show us ourselves as well as any process.

3. The next step is up to the student. As individual students discover the darkness that is within each of us—elements Jung has called the "shadow"—and also intimations of the self, they will likely want to turn inward to confront these realities within themselves. It is one situation to see these elements in others in the group. But when one turns inward, one finds that there are dark and destructive forces bearing in upon him directly, demonic forces which he cannot control by himself.

Then the teacher's example and reassurance are needed. He must let the student know, in the way that speaks to that individual and his type, that one is not alone. Others have found that rational consciousness cannot handle these forces, and have sought some power other than the human. In this way, the student may find his or her need to encounter the creative Spirit manifested by Christ, and thus turn for support to this reality which Christ gave to the church to use.

We have already emphasized that this inner journey is no joy ride, and that one encounters not only elements that change according to how one deals with them, but also an aspect or content that seems to be ultimately destructive. This content, which drives men to illness and psychosis, Jung has described in terrifying detail. Those who actually meet this reality must find some help other than human, or they are lost. Religion then becomes more than a nice additive to a well-balanced life. The teacher who has to deal with this depth of the individual must be aware of the dangers, and at least comfortable with taking religion this seriously himself. Then he will not be frightened by what the student experiences. This very calmness and assurance, on its own, has tremendous power.

There is probably no limit to the depth and variety of individual discovery that can be made, or the ways it can be used. There are some things written on this, including those by Jung. But in the particular situation the qualities of the teacher are determining. As we look at what is required of Christian educators, let us remember that their own growth is also involved in this process.

4. A good teacher will know these inner realities well enough not to be threatened by the hostility which a student may express in any direction in the group. Even more important, the teacher will not be threatened by the positive caring which such a situation can constellate. The atmosphere within the class, and whether the group is left in unresolved hostility or moves towards caring, depend upon the leader, and often on his ability to seek help himself.

The educator's conscious attitudes are not the only factor, however. One's unconscious attitudes also play an important part in what students actually take from the learning process. If teachers are aware of their own unconsciousness and of the forces that can play upon them from the spiritual world, they can begin to know what other attitudes they are imparting to their students along with the conscious ones. Teachers need to know whether they are reenforcing their teaching unconsciously, or if they sometimes impart unconsciously the opposite of what is intended; this is particularly true in teaching religion.

5. A teacher will be professional in the sense that he or she is not in the teaching position to satisfy one's own needs (and this takes a lot of consciousness). The teacher will remain the

catalyst, a part of the reaction and yet outside it, ready to be withdrawn once it has taken place. Students need their freedom, and they need the security of knowing that the teacher is there *when he is needed.* As the individual comes to his own ground, the teacher withdraws. He may not even be appreciated by the students. His influence will be seen by only the most perceptive, and few will realize what he has done to set up and maintain a climate of experiential learning.

6. Teachers will also be professional in understanding their subject matter. They will have done their intellectual homework, as well as the developmental kind, so that they have an integrated understanding of *content* and how it relates to their own experiences and the experiences of the various groups. The teacher—in class or home, who is trying to communicate religion in a specific way—will know what he believes and why he believes in that way.

7. One very important quality of such a teacher is the confidence which he or she sometimes feels—and sometimes only expresses as best one can in words and actions—that there is a creative power in the universe, a power best expressed in Christ and his Spirit, which seeks to enter into relationship with the individual, to protect and guide each of us towards wholeness and meaning.

Finally, there are the tools of the trade. The Bible is one which the church has provided for religious education. There is no greater help than this book when it is seen as the history of God's encounter with human beings. From the beginning the elements are there that one finds in himself, and most of our ways of encountering and dealing with them. In their culmination one finds the unsurpassed personality of Jesus Christ, the whole man in whom God broke through. The stories, the teachings and actions of Christ give direction to the individual search once they are seen as a guide and not as a strait jacket. In the resurrection there is the knowledge that the world was unable to destroy the whole God-man, and this gives us the hope that there is a new life, and a great destiny, for those whose lives are open to the inflow of his Spirit.

In addition there is the history of the church, a history of numerous encounters of God with men and women from the end of the New Testament until the present. As the lives of Augustine, St. Francis, Martin Luther, St. Catherine of Siena, William Law, Thomas Kelly, all show, revelation continues, and human beings are still touched and changed. If the point of view we have presented is correct, these individuals have left a record of encounter which is second in importance for our guidance only to the Biblical narrative.

The liturgy is the other, double-pronged tool. In it the church acts out its own continued care for each of us within the family of Christ. At the same time, as Christ's central act of caring is remembered and reenacted in the way that he suggested, he is present in continuing reality, expressed in and through the fellowship and the bread and wine. Classroom teaching can be a preparation for this experience, which itself is one of the finest ways the church communicates its message. A real liturgy, when seen in depth, is teaching par excellence.

Summary

The Christian church is needed by people today probably more than ever before in its history. For this reason we are going over some difficult ground in these pages in order to see how Christians can effectively tap and communicate the power that should be theirs to offer people who need it. To sum up, these are the suggestions I am trying to support and give body to. It is up to each of us to make them live.

1. There is a religious reality about which individuals desperately need to know if they are to survive and grow in our twentieth century world. This is at least as important as any other area of learning.

2. The knowledge of this reality—like any other knowledge, scientific, mathematical, or religious—is given through experience. Our reason, our logic and rational thought are essential in order to understand our experiences, which are never given with absolute, predictable certainty. But, in spite of the understanding of some recent philosophy and theology, it is not our logic or rational thought that give us knowledge of any kind. If

individuals are to know God, they must go back again and again to their experiences of the divine and find the knowledge that God gives to those who seek.

3. It is impossible to find this knowledge measured and packaged for ready consumption. The spiritual world requires an individual response from each of us. God requires a more personal, a more individual interaction from those who would learn of him than do the objects of chemistry or physics or geology. Learning about God is more like learning about another human being than about things, and human beings seldom reveal themselves until the conditions are right. If God had been able to communicate himself through a law or prescription, he very likely would have done so. But there seems to be no easy, mass method of arriving at mature religious practice. Once this is deeply understood and accepted, we will not be taken in by one panacea or another, but will be ready to give the effort that is needed to know God.

God himself came as a person in Jesus of Nazareth, whose ministry was not limited to one way of communication. It was a ministry of exemplification, joined with acts of power and creative love, and with teaching. It was communication in the fullest sense. It resulted in a conflict with evil and death, and finally in resurrection. This was all part of the way God taught his message in Jesus Christ. God himself made a great effort. It is not our task to imitate all of this, but we need to do more than just talk about it or draw up propositional statements to be memorized. There is a Spirit which can live in and through our lives if we allow it, the Spirit sent by Jesus Christ.

4. Our central task in the church is to know and communicate this Spirit. But since the church has failed to provide either an encounter with this Spirit or the understanding that would lead to it, we must first develop the intellectual understanding and the emotional and spiritual conditions that will allow experiences of the Holy Spirit to work in and give value to our own lives. With this theological, psychological, and philosophical base, we can then get on with the task of communicating religion.

5. Genuine communication of religion, as an individualized

undertaking, will try to express concern for the individual and his growth. Only so much of man's religious potential can be achieved in youth, or at any other single stage. Religious education is a lifelong venture. Yet much of the basic learning about religion comes to us as children from our parents. Thus for two reasons—for our own growth and for our influence on our children—the importance of communicating knowledge of religious realities to adults can hardly be overestimated.

In addition, one comes to know the realities with which religion deals in an individual encounter, and since the forces in the religious encounter are so complex, this communication will take place in small groups.

6. Religious education is the most demanding kind of teaching. It requires insight, consciousness, and continuing growth on the part to the teacher. One has to know not only the subject matter, and something of the experiences and the world view that support it, but also a great deal about the learner and his dynamics as well. One will see himself more a catalyst, stimulating reaction within the learner and among the group, than as a reacting part of the process. This requires the greatest self-understanding and maturity.

Let us turn now to the Christian goal of maturity and wholeness of personality, asking how we can understand human personality so as to help others on this way.

5

Education for Wholeness

*The way we understand the nature of the person to be edu-
cated will determine to a large extent just how we conceive
the nature of the educational process and how we go about
practicing it.*

Now and then one hears about some lucky students, in high
school or college, who make contact with a teacher so challenging that their lives are changed. Decisions are made, lives are
directed toward fulfilling goals, and parents and friends marvel
at what happens in that classroom. Then one day there is a
retirement party, and when the eulogies die away, people find
that they have learned little, if anything, about what makes such
a great teacher. The teacher may not even know, for he or she
may never have reflected upon the actions and life style which
could draw even mediocre students into the education process.

Most people, in fact, simply do not reflect upon their ways of
reacting to other human beings. But there is more than one
reason for those who are interested in religious education to do
so. Almost all of us have some dominant pattern of reacting to
others. If we reflect upon that pattern, trying to see and bring
out all that is usually taken for granted, and then state the results
of our reflection as clearly as possible, what we arrive at is called
our theory of personality. Developing such a theory is like snap-
ping a variety of pictures, working with the negatives, and finally
putting together an album that actually shows something about
family life.

When people do not reflect in this way, they still operate on a
kind of theory. But their theory of personality is implicit or
assumed. It is taken for granted, since they do not think much

about their behavior or consider all the assumptions and ideas on which they base their actions. Usually such a pattern of action has been picked up from the culture of which these people are a part, and they keep acting on it even though they may *say* something quite different about human beings. In fact, the actual theory of personality on which a person operates is revealed far more by his actions than by what he *says* or what he *thinks* he thinks about the nature of human personality. Actions do speak louder than words when it comes to telling about the basic ideas upon which we direct our actions.

For several reasons it is important for each of us to express our personality theory. In the first place, if an implicit theory is inadequate, there is no way of getting hold of it to criticize it or alter it. New understandings about personality cannot readily be integrated into an unstated position. In addition, we can never be really sure about any of the beliefs that underlie our actions unless they can be expressed and examined. We may be sitting on a powder keg of ideas that contradict everything we would like other people to believe and base their actions on. The ideas we hold in the depth of our being are important. In fact we human beings are quite consistent in the long run; we usually act out what we really believe.

Then there are the problems that can be caused when a person holds two divergent attitudes implicitly, or when some attitude implicitly held differs from one's stated view about how human beings act. Until both are stated there is no way of reconciling or integrating them. Those who have worked with disturbed people know the confusion that is caused by parents who are caught between different patterns of reaction. Indeed, any pattern of action which is implicit and not stated controls the individual; he does not direct or control it, *or* his actions. And when there is a multiplicity of different reaction patterns or little consistent pattern at all in an individual, that person is usually called unstable or sick and is excluded from the social group.

Finally, it is of utmost importance for Christian educators to realize how much the goals and direction of education depend upon our basic theory of personality. *The way we understand the nature of the person to be educated will determine to a large extent just how we conceive the nature of the educational process and how we go about practicing it.* There are a number of ways in which one can view human personality and its capacity for experience. Any one of them that is commonly held, whether conscious or implicit, is likely to exert a strong influence on every activity devoted to human beings, including how we direct our educational plans and practices.

Probably the most widely held idea of personality at present is the implicit theory that was discussed in the last chapter. Let us review this idea briefly and then look at the most developed and adequate theory of which I am aware, one that is conscious and tries to encompass the actual diversities of human behavior. Then we shall take a good look at the value of such an understanding of personality for Christian education.

A Widely Held View of Personality

As we have seen, this is a simplified view of human beings. This theory is also very difficult to deal with because it is held for the most part by people who see no reason whatever to examine their belief in it. They are quite sure that our personalities are formed of conscious and rational elements, and that it is easy to see how the environment places these elements in each human being. Each of us, it is assumed, starts life as a blank page or a vessel empty of any psychic stuff, waiting to be filled by our life experiences.

Our society has the task of arranging for the kind of education that will fill the growing individual with experiences carefully selected to build up an acceptable and useful personality. The role of educators becomes well defined. Their purpose is to understand the goals of society, select the right pattern (perhaps the educator's own pattern), and then administer a system of feeding information, rewards, and punishments that will produce socially acceptable, law-abiding citizens. Once the personalities have been properly shaped, the educator has no further responsibilities. It is up to society to see that the pattern is maintained. If a person does not turn out right—either because education failed to provide the right experiences or because of a defect in the person's will—there are other institutions to take over. Their job is mainly to correct the individual and alter his will by punishment. And if even this fails, then the community has no choice but to remove that person from the group so that his unhealthy behavior will not harm or infect others.

Once again, I have made no effort to show these ideas in their true perspective. They can have real value, of course, when their use is balanced and tempered by other methods of education which develop out of a less one-sided understanding of human beings. As I have suggested, however, most of our law courts, prisons, mental institutions, and even many families and schools have operated for a long time almost exclusively on these principles. The results have been shown in various studies, particularly of prison methods and of mental health problems. In addition there is no way of reducing to statistics the damage done by families that take this approach to the individual members, or by the failure of this theory of personality to offer much, if any, understanding of mental disturbance, either psychotic or neurotic.

Nevertheless, this point of view still exerts a tremendous hold on most unreflective people, and anyone who challenges it meets with determined resistance. It is like challenging the person's religion. This is much the same attitude as that of the Old Testament, as expressed in Proverbs and by the deuteronomic editors. Up to the flowering of Greek culture in the Socratic period, this was essentially the theory of the ancient world, and it was later handed down to Western thinkers through Aristotle and Aquinas. It has been the basis of the legal codes of nearly all cultures and ages, and also of most ecclesiastical censure. It has recently been revived as a theory of personality and restated with sophistication by certain modern psychologists.

In recent years, as men have become more aware of emotional disturbance and unacceptable behavior, some students of human nature have suggested other points of view. The most fruitful of these conceptions, from my experience, suggests that man's behavior is not determined just by his consciously held ideas, but also by the contents of what is called the unconscious. The idea of the unconscious itself is a relatively recent development. L. L. Whyte has pointed out that the word *unconscious* as a noun did not even occur in Western languages until after Descartes had defined thought as a clear, conscious, rational process, obviously leaving something out. Descartes came to his understanding in a way that was hardly a clear, conscious, rational process—through a triple dream experience on the night of November 10, 1619. Yet ironically, he did not seem to notice that he had overlooked anything of importance for understanding human personality.

Others did, however; and gradually the idea of the unconscious grew—more or less like Topsy until Freud's discovery of the principle of psychic causation and of the dream as a tool for delving into the contents of the unconscious. At this point Carl Jung's investigations began.

A Workable Theory of Personality

My knowledge of Jung's thinking, first of all, gave me an hypothesis in terms of which I was able to solve many of my own personal problems; and second, I have seen others reach similar solutions by using the same framework in mutual discussion. Thus I have seen this hypothesis verified again and again. I have also found that this psychological point of view is quite similar to the understanding of personality which is the foundation of the teaching and practice of Jesus of Nazareth, and so it has important religious implications. Like many other aspects of the teaching of Jesus—the rights of women, social justice, freedom from slavery—this understanding took centuries before it began to bear fruit. It can also be supported philosophically.

This approach to the development of personality, that pays the unconscious its due, can be presented in a model or schema like this:

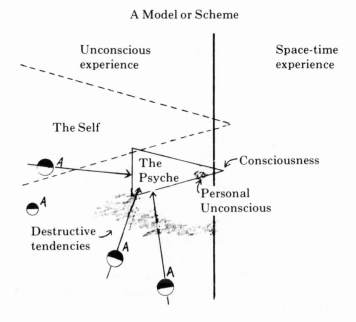

A Model or Scheme

The central triangle represents the human psyche with its tip of consciousness extending into the physical world on right of the central line. The elements of the unconscious (or spiritual) world are represented on the left.

Such a diagram obviously has the same faults as a word picture. It is oversimplified and maps the territory just about as an oil company map of Colorado shows what is in Rocky Mountain Park. But the advantage is that it does try to represent the most developed points of C. G. Jung's thinking in a form appropriate to a short discussion. His thinking continued to develop right up to his death. The evidence for it is found in the nineteen volumes of his collected works. Let us look at the most important points along this road, simply describing them, of course, since it is not possible in such a summary to produce the evidence or develop the very important rationale for them.

1. Usually one first becomes aware of the unconscious when

one realizes that some content which had been conscious has slipped away from recall and then inexplicably comes to mind. Or a forgotten attitude becomes today's willful desire. One cannot say that such contents have disappeared, for they often exert influence upon a person when he or she is least aware that they exist. In fact, neurosis can sometimes be resolved simply by recalling and dealing with contents like these. Much of our behavior is the result of the pressure of these contents of the *personal unconscious;* a slip of the tongue, a missed appointment, other errors often clearly betray the connection.

2. In addition to contents that were once conscious and have been repressed, there also seem to be those with no derivative relationship to the individual ego. In some of his last published pages and in the later *Moses and Monotheism* and *Totem and Taboo,* Freud wrote about discovering something in the unconscious besides repressed memories and the strictly wish-fulfilling activity of the id. He saw primal traces, what he called racial memories, which he distinguished mostly as atavistic, destructive tendencies operating within the unconscious. Jung and his followers continued to study this aspect of the unconscious and to amass information about it.

Jung had patients from all over the world, and it was startling to find how many correspondences there were in the unconscious materials of all these people. He also found distinguishable common contents which appeared to impinge upon the human psyche that did not originate either in the space-time world or in human consciousness. These contents he called *archetypes.* Often they appeared in combination with elements from the personal unconscious. Or sometimes they broke in autonomously with almost no personal content. Since this appears most distinctly in the dream and the vision, there was evidence available about these elements. This evidence forced Jung to believe that there are creative contents that break in upon man which are superior to human consciousness, as well as contents that are inferior or primitive.

While the evidence for the archetypal aspect of unconscious contents is much less common than ordinary unconscious experience, even so it is somewhat more accessible than the evidence for the disintegration of the atom. There are recent examples. One of them—*The Teachings of Don Juan* by Carlos Castaneda—describes how the Yaqui Indians use peyote to bring contact with the same world. Other examples are found in the scientific studies compiled by Charles Tart in his book, *Altered States of Consciousness*, as well as in Jung's writings, particularly *Memories, Dreams, Reflections*.

The evidence also brought Jung to the conclusion that the individual comes into life with a psychic inheritance and structure, as well as a biological one. Each of us starts with certain archetypal configurations which give one a unique quality as a person. Each psyche is also oriented towards these forms, as well as towards the outer world, by an innate structure or type.

3. Thus Jung sees man as caught between two worlds—a world of space and time which is experienced through the five senses, and a world of nonphysical reality which he calls the *collective unconscious* or the *objective psyche*. The clearest statement I have seen of this viewpoint came in a letter he wrote to me in 1958, acknowledging that we do not understand the world beyond, but it is an experiential fact. In it there are numerous archetypal contents that are of ambivalent nature, depending on how the individual deals with them. There is one aspect or element, however, which seems to be ultimately destructive, driving men to illness and psychosis. This kind of content is depicted by the witches in *Macbeth*, by Mephistopheles in Faust, and by the evil one so accurately described in the witchcraft in the film *Rosemary's Baby*. Jung describes this *destructive element* with terrifying reality in the sixth chapter of his book, *Memories, Dreams, Reflections*.

He was far more interested, however, in the creative, restoring aspect of the unconscious, the integrative complex which he called the *self* and described in works like *Psychology and Alchemy, Aion*, and others. Dealing directly with these realities requires dedication, courage, and even suffering. It involves the whole man. In his discussions of these aspects one sees that Jung's statements often represent stages in fifty years of developing ideas, and that they should be read in the light of his latest and most mature understanding.

Jung maintained that he was not describing ideas, but psychic contents which could be discovered empirically by anyone who would take the trouble to investigate. Father Hostie in his book on Jung has described his method as that of "nonexperimental empiricism." In fact, unless one deals with the experiences Jung has described, judging his findings is about like criticizing the theories of nuclear physics without knowing any mathematics or the use of a cloud chamber. Jung wrote from experience, his own and that of patients from all over the world. He described a variety of experience known and described by most religious people of every time and place, particularly by the church fathers up to Aquinas. These men called it experience of the spiritual world, and they did quite a bit of writing about its positive and negative contents, and what it cost the individual to encounter and deal with them.

4. The task of psychological therapy is to make the individual aware of his own unique psychic structure and his relation to this storehouse of unconscious contents, releasing him from bondage to the negative ones and helping him relate to the creative and integrative aspects in it. The therapist then is a midwife, not one who creates in his own image. But he has a job to do, knowing experientially the structure of the unconscious, the darkness that is encountered, and something of the intimations of the self that can come. As the individual stands against the forces of darkness within him and feels himself alienated from others, he knows depression, perhaps neurotic flight or withdrawal into ideas of reference, even a manic state, or denial of reality by a dissolution of the ego. The therapist walks through this darkness with him, having withstood it himself, and allows this one, this individual, to seek his own unique, creative meaning among the realities of the objective psyche. This is essentially a learning process.

There is another very important element; if anything, the crucial element. This is not a process characterized by detachment and lack of personal involvement. Quite to the contrary, it is seldom possible without a deep concern for the other person, the individual involved in the encounter. Jung describes this element as transference; he wrote about it in one of his more difficult essays, "The Psychology of the Transference." In one of the concluding paragraphs of his autobiography he implied that only as one is possessed by love can one know the reality of the self and enable another to find it. James Hillman has expressed the same experience well in *Suicide and the Soul*.

This involves the whole person. Just as the entire person, conscious and unconscious, of a mother or teacher affects the child, so the entire personality of the therapist has an influence upon the patient. The New Testament put it rather well, that one gets into this other realm by becoming as a little child, even a new-born baby, who often reacts more to the unconscious attitudes and desires of the parents than to their conscious frame of reference. Or, from the completely negative side, as Jung often remarked, Hitler's power rose from the effect of his unconscious on the unconscious of the German people without much mediation through conscious channels. Jung was as interested in the so-called normal personality as in the pathological, and his theory refers as significantly to ordinary men and women as it does to people who wander into a therapist's office to be relieved of symptoms.

Those who have been brought up in either materialistic or scholastic rationalism usually find this point of view anything but congenial. However, it can be supported philosophically. If one accepts the basic epistemology of Plato instead of that of Aristotle—if one grants that man has relationship with the non-physical realm, not through reason, but by direct encounter in four ways, particularly through love—then this point of view is not absurd at all, but makes sense of the evidence. This was the general attitude of the church fathers that was brought to clear expression in Augustine.

If one can consider the basic dualism of Kant—which sees man in touch with a real physical world and a real mental world, but with no certain, final knowledge about either one—then again this view is not absurd. According to Kant, phenomenal experience is the result of the interaction of a noumenal object and noumenal subjects, and can refer to either.

Jung's approach extends the consideration of the experience of the subject to include the nonrational aspects of the subject or psyche. Thus the human psyche's phenomenal experience includes the contents of the unconscious—dreams, intuitions, religious experience—as well as the purely conscious and rational contents of this aspect of experience. Jung's point of view is that of a pragmatic realist in which two real and experientially different kinds of phenomenal experience are available to us: an experience of a physical world, and an experience of a nonphysical or psychic world. Both kinds of experience have important and observable effects upon the individual. Each kind of experience gives contact with a perceptibly different reality, each of which can be described and increasingly understood as our reasoning function is turned towards it. At present there is insufficient evidence to reduce these two realms to one for the sake of logical tidiness.

This point of view is quite in accord with the world view of Jesus and the early church. The New Testament teaching about *charismata,* or gifts, has a place. Spiritual gifts can be understood as the way the creative aspect of nonphysical reality works through the individual—in healings, dreams and visions, supernatural knowledge, the distinguishing of the angelic and demonic (or creative and destructive aspects of archetypal contents), and prophecy, tongues and interpretation, which are all of major concern in the New Testament.

Some Basic Implications for Education

There are many implications of this view of personality. It touches nearly every aspect of man's life. Not only are there religious and philosophical implications, but also medical and therapeutic. This point of view sheds much light on the understanding of art, drama, and literature. There are also implications that can be seen in the political and social field, and in the broader aspects of industrial and economic relations. And there are the educational implications. It is to these that we now turn.

1. If there actually are two realms of phenomenal reality, an education that considers only one of them is inadequate. It fails to help the individual find an approach or a means of dealing with one whole aspect of human experience, and this has very practical results. When we do not deal directly with the unconscious aspects of this psychic reality, we usually project them out onto other people and try to deal with them in outer relationships. This is seldom creative. Unconscious projection is responsible for the cults of hate, of war, racism, and revolution. It results in the cult of romantic love which so often keeps people from relating to the real individual. The alchemists took a different tack and projected their unconscious psychic contents into matter. They did not provide much valuable chemical information, although they did provide the modern analytical psychologist with a happy hunting ground of psychic material.

It is no easy matter to learn to deal with these unconscious contents. One needs help and training to keep to a narrow, tortuous path, often in the darkness that most people run from. It takes as much effort and care as dealing witn subatomic particles. This is different from the broad collective way people follow when they are unaware of the unconscious. There are tools, however, for discovering the nature of this aspect of experience. The dream, as Jung, Freud, and the doctors of the church have shown, is the simplest and most accessible, and there are other creative ways to help each individual use the experiences that come to him through his psyche. This, of course, is subject enough for several discussions.

2. If the individual human being enters life with his own psychic inheritance and structure, then education must be something different from putting formless psychic stuff into a mold. Instead, the task of education is to allow the forces of creativity to emerge in the way that is unique for that individual. Its purpose is to provide the circumstances in which the individual may grow to the maximum of his potential within the opportunities at hand. Here I have lifted the phrases—with which I agree—of the industrialist friend I have spoken of who built his business on this conception of his task.

One seldom creates these conditions through hostility or punishment, but rather by concern, love, *agape*. Hostility usually evokes the negative and destructive forces latent in the person, making him draw on his inner defensive powers, rather than releasing the creative aspects of the unconscious. Thus the atmosphere of interested concern, even when setting and maintaining limits, is vital to this conception of education. Anger and rejection scarcely lead to the greatest development, the unfolding of the individual.

3. It is important for the growing individual to discover his own pattern if he is to make his unique contribution. There are many different types of individuals, and each has his own unique value. Jung's type theory gives a theoretical basis for understanding the value of different human beings from the point of view of the unconscious. According to his understanding human beings are essentially either extraverted or introverted, and are dominant in either thinking, feeling, intuition, or sensation. Our modern society puts a premium on the extraverted thinking + sensation type. It is helpful for those who are not extraverted thinkers simply to realize that there are other types which are not necessarily inferior.

Knowledge of the individual's strengths, and also his weakness, through type testing, is an important tool for guidance in education. Type structure can affect motivation, and a lot of research needs to be done on this little understood subject. It is perhaps even more important to understand possible type structure so as to discover one's own type and learn about others in the interaction of the learning group. Along with his objective learning, the individual can learn to value persons, including himself, as they are.

4. The unconscious attitudes of the teacher play an important part in the actual learning process, as well as his conscious attitudes. As I have suggested, there is just one way to find out what attitudes the students may be picking up without our intending it. That is to make contact with the unconscious and learn all that we can about the contents that are actually playing into the psyche and how they are affecting us. Of course it is possible for the unconscious to support one's conscious pur-

poses. But the things that need to be taught in religious education make it very dangerous to rely on this possibility. Teaching about love, for instance, will not be very effective if it happens to be accompanied by a demonstration of unconscious anger.

One of my sons for a time attended an Episcopal parochial school. His teacher was a nun whose outer conscious attitude was that of warmth and concern, a delightful "Christian" person. Underneath was an opinionated and power-driven animus. This was the most negative experience this boy ever had with religion and the church. Again, exactly the opposite may be true. The priest who taught chemistry for a time at Groton school used to tell me with a twinkle in his eye how religion ought to be taught. Teaching chemistry with his collar on, saying nothing about religion, and caring how and what his students learned, he said, was more effective in conveying religious instruction than most of the courses in religion at the school.

The teacher-student relationship is an archetypally powerful one. If the student is really intent upon learning, he has dropped his defenses and is open to what the teacher is. Is it not almost as important for the educator to be aware of and working with his own unconscious conflicts and complexes as it is for the therapist?

Dealing with the unconscious is no easier for the educator than for the therapist. Confrontation with the unconscious is always a difficult and dangerous undertaking, and it is certainly not to be recommended for everyone. But if one's primary vocational task is dealing with others and attempting to educate them, can one avoid this difficult undertaking without seriously interfering with one's goal? The safest way of dealing with the unconscious I have been able to discover is within the framework and context of our religion.

5. Once one realizes, perhaps experiences, the reality of the unconscious as we have been considering it, the individual is then seen in relationship, not only with a space-time material world, but also with an equally vast, nonphysical realm of experience which is not governed by space and time. We are in contact with certain contents that give value and meaning to life.

They are the very source of value itself. No one is cut off from these contents because of intellectual or social status. Each individual is valuable, and thus no one is just a thing, something expendable. Each person, according to this point of view, must be given the opportunity to develop and to contribute to the maximum of his unique capacities.

This kind of thinking is diametrically opposed to that of Aristotle, who assumed a different value for certain men. In reasoning about dreams, he concluded that they could not come from the gods because simple peasants received just as significant dreams as did intelligent and rational men. Obviously the gods would never send revelations to simple people, but only to the rational and highly intelligent who could use them. Aristotle assumed that the gods concurred in his valuation of one certain type of human being. I have sometimes wondered where I would measure with Aristotle.

6. Finally, one of the most central and important contents of experience reached through the unconscious is what Jung called the self. The ultimate development of the human being, his individuation or wholeness, depends upon his awareness of this content of the unconscious—this aspect of nonphysical or spiritual reality—and his interaction with it. Relationship with this creative center is a religious process whether one chooses to call it by that name or not.

The unconscious has vast religious and theological implications. Education which enables a person to deal with the whole of life, physical and nonphysical, necessarily then has religious implications. Education like this can bring one into contact with God, as well as with the split-off and negative elements of experience. It would be well for each of us to examine consciously how our personality theory correlates with our religious ideas and experiences.

We have presented a model of human personality in which the unconscious is an essential ingredient. If this model does indeed reflect the reality of the human being, then the unconscious, as considered by Jung, has implications for nearly every aspect of human behavior. There are almost as many implications for education as there are for psychotherapy, perhaps more if one considers the preventive aspects and also the relation of young people to this reality today. Youngsters today are getting into the unconscious on their own, spontaneously, or else by hook or crook, with or without drugs, when it does not break through without an assist. Thus the unconscious, both personal and collective, is inextricably involved in education—in the process itself, in its scope, direction, and meaning—and also in the educators themselves, one hopes, by choice.

How, then, do emotions fit into our understanding of personality, and what place do these often troublesome reactions have in our plans and schemes for educating Christians?

6

Education for Understanding Emotion and Finding Value

Not too many subjects are in a more confused state today than the matter of human emotions—except perhaps religion. Surveying the literature on the subject, I find myself more sympathetic than ever with my own up-tight generation and with religious educators. Let us start, then, by looking at two attitudes towards the place of affect or emotion in human life. These two attitudes, which represent almost diametrically opposed ideas about the value of our emotions, are both current today and both tugging at us for attention.

One one hand, emotional reactions are seen as a disordered and destructive human response; the very words emotion, affect, affectivity are derogatory terms. And on the other, many psychologists and educators have come to see that if either adults or children are to function adequately in their various life situations, they need some ways of understanding and using affect. Let us first examine the points of view that see emotionality only as a negative entity. We shall next look at quite a different view, and then try to define the human response that is being viewed. Then let us try to understand what is involved in affectivity, how it functions, and finally ask if there are ways of using emotion which have meaning for the teaching of religion.

Two Opposite Attitudes

Two contributors to the first symposium on feelings and emotions, held at Clark University in 1927 expressed very pointedly the attitude that affect is meaningless and simply disruptive. D. T. Howard, a psychologist from Northwestern University, remarked,

> I have always been interested in that question, as to the value of emotional states, and the conclusion to which I come is that they have absolutely no value at all, but represent a defect in human nature.

The University of Chicago psychologist, Harvey A. Carr, expressed the same conviction:

> The biological utility of the emotions . . . has been somewhat overemphasized. In order to promote survival, perhaps Nature would have been wiser to have endowed organisms with less emotion and more cunning and intelligence.

Although these statements were both made before 1930, this attitude has not died out in the meantime. James Hillman in his comprehensive survey of the literature, *Emotion: A Comprehensive Phenomenology of Theories and Their Meanings for Therapy*, commented in 1964 that

> The divorce of emotion and reason is now so long-standing and has worked so to the benefit of reason that emotion has become by definition in most textbooks—as well as in common speech—a pejorative concept of irrationality bordering on the insane. The exclusion of emotion from the temples of art, science, religion, law, and moral philosophy, leaves it little recourse but to appear where it has been driven, in the marketplaces and alley-ways of crime, mobs, war and the asylum.

Hillman cites a recent study by Franklin Fearing, covering nine textbooks on social psychology, showing how generally emotion is dismissed or disparaged.

Besides this attitude, there is the picture drawn by the behaviorists, who see affect with no autonomy or meaning beyond its physical manifestations in specific behavior. The logical positivists and linguistic analysts follow along because they cannot logically prove that the idea of emotion has reality. It makes non-sense as a concept, and a meaningless myth like this does not deserve serious intellectual study. The result is that many writers have considered emotion the ghost in the machine, as Gilbert Ryle put it in his *Concept of Mind*, specifying that impulses, described as feelings which impel action, are "paramechanical myths." In the 1927 symposium previously mentioned, Knight Dunlap of Johns Hopkins stated that

> The so-called emotions of the psychologist... remain, however, in the world of myth. They are, so far as I can understand, neither objects nor occurrences, nor relations, but mystical entities, concerning which a mass of mystical speculation has grown up.... They have the same connection with reality as the hypogriff, the demon, and the entelechy.

With this general attitude at work in much of our intellectual community, it is no wonder that a real understanding of affect, or emotion, has been so long in gaining acceptance and that the subject is so often approached with trepidation. Still, there are men of intellect today—men who deal with human beings in the handling of their practical affairs—who have discovered that the subject of emotion cannot be avoided.

Beginning with the pioneering work of Sigmund Freud at the start of our century, most psychotherapists have found the notion of affect useful; in fact they have been able to help patients deal with neurotic and psychotic disturbances only as they have learned to understand and deal with both conscious and hidden emotional life. In addition, the studies initiated by Dr. Flanders Dunbar in her pivotal book, *Emotions and Bodily Changes*, indicate that the human body, as well as the human personality, can suffer permanent physical damage through emotions which are untamed, often not even recognized.

In recent years educators have come to see that the emotional climate of the classroom is one of the important variables in the learning situation. Studies by some of the most respected empirical researchers in education—people like Ned Flanders at Ann Arbor, Marie Hughes, and Hugh Perkins, the author of *Human Development and Learning*—give evidence that even cognitive learning is helped along by a creative emotional climate generated by the teacher's affectivity. This suggestion did not surprise me, even though the results are not considered conclusive in regard to intellectual learning.

In the psychological work done for people in my former parish, we discovered something that is well known among many psychologists—that severe anxiety has a measurable negative effect upon I.Q. and can change the adult scores. In many cases once the anxiety was dealt with, students who had had serious learning problems found they no longer had such problems, and began to make unexpected progress.

There is general agreement about the need for a favorable emotional climate for learning related to conduct, action, and value. This learning can hardly be facilitated at all by purely cognitive methods; affectivity is a necessary ingredient. One authority proposes that learning so as to change behavior is most likely to occur when the experiences take place in a situation which frees the learner from any sense of personal threat, so that he or she interacts with others in a wholesome social milieu. William H. Stavsky goes even further in his article, "Using the Insights of Psychotherapy in Teaching," holding that the teacher's ability to recognize the needs of the child

> . . . will depend on the significance he attributes to the emotional factor in learning. If he agrees that learning is as much a matter of feeling as it is of brains, the obvious implication is that the teacher must continue to add to his teaching skills an increasing professional understanding of the psychology of maladjustment. The effect . . . is a significant gain for the teaching and learning process.

If these psychological and educational authorities know what they are talking about, then it behooves us who are the teachers—particularly those who teach religion and want to see it put into practice—to understand the dynamics of emotionality as well as we can.

Towards a Definition of Emotion and Affect

Everyone has some idea of what is meant by the word emotion, but when we come to pin down a precise definition of affect or emotion, we find that we are dealing with a very complex human reaction, which is almost as difficult to describe as sleep or dreaming.

We might identify it off-hand as a state of consciousness, known inwardly, and characterized by fear or anxiety, hate or anger, love or affection. It is an aspect of human life that has to do with desiring, wanting or not wanting, and action in reaction, and it is distinguished from another inwardly known activity known as thought or cognition. Affect directly stimulates a total human response or reaction, in contrast to cognitive processes which stimulate only the intellect. Affect is also known as the diffused state of reaction, resulting from emotional stimulation, which involves a human being on nearly every level of his being. The words affect and emotion refer to the same aspect of human life, although affect has a slightly more reputable and scientific connotation, and they can be used interchangeably.

How, then, do we describe the person's affective life? How does an emotion function? It is not hard to see that we are trying to describe one of the most fundamental and elusive aspects of human nature, one that is just about as hard to pigeonhole as life itself.

Emotional reactions are obviously more complex than purely cognitive or intellectual ones; the whole human organism is involved. Both the conscious and the unconscious areas of personality are brought into play. At least two areas of the brain—the cortex and the thalamus—are involved. An incredibly complicated set of glandular and physiological reactions takes place as the autonomic nervous system begins to function. Through the central nervous system and the blood stream, the whole chemical balance and the organic and muscular system of the body suddenly react—from heart, lungs, stomach, and so on, to skeletal muscles. Affectivity is an all-inclusive response, a response of the whole human being, both psychic and physical. Most theories of emotion have seized upon one aspect of this complex human reaction and have reduced emotion to the single aspect that interested the author. This is particularly true of innovators who discovered some new manifestation or other.

There are so many bodily manifestations that many theorists have been inclined to see emotion as nothing more than consciousness of an altered physical state. The James-Lange theory regarded emotion in this way. Therefore, when one consciously changed his physical attitude and stance—for instance if one simply whistled when afraid—one could actually change his emotional state. But it became apparent that even in animals more is involved than this. Many of the somatic effects of emotion were discovered to result from the activation of the involuntary nervous system, and it was realized that, through consciousness and rationality alone, it is practically impossible to control affectivity.

When the nervous system is activated by fear or anger, an autonomic reaction takes place. The innervation (which may well involve electronic reactions) passes from the thalamus to the pituitary gland; the adrenal glands are thereby stimulated; the bronchial tubes are opened to allow in more oxygen for a greater release of energy; the tissues and liver release blood sugar; the clotting time of the blood is decreased; blood flow to the viscera is reduced; the skeletal muscles tighten; heartbeat is speeded up; blood pressure increases; and, among various other things, the electrical conductivity of the skin changes by measurable amounts.

As the lie detector demonstrates, these reactions can occur apart from any physical cause. Simply the presentation of emotionally charged ideas to the mind of a subject produces the changes that are charted. But if one believes that only physical reactions are involved, then the approach to emotional disturbances is limited. Understanding them then hinges on the success or failure of shock treatment, positive thinking, or methods like water therapy, rest, games, drill, and now chemical therapy. Yet probably the most effective method that has been found for limiting emotional response is the practice of yoga exercises, demonstrated by Choisy in his sophisticated experiments in India.

Looked at from the point of view of its outer meaning, affect is characterized by conflict. It is the response of the individual when ordinary and accustomed patterns of reacting no longer suffice. When habitual and rational responses fail to work and one does not know how to respond, emotion arises. The conflict may be between the individual and his outer environment, or it may come from his identifying with one aspect of an outer situation. Emotion can also arise from conflict within the individual, as between opposing goals and desires, or between different levels of personality.

When the individual is caught within a conflicting situation, emotion represents a massive discharge of vital energy which breaks him out of his accustomed patterns. For this reason, from the point of view of society and the ego, emotion has been considered a factor in most change, and even in the alteration of a train of ideas. Thus Sartre has described emotion as man's magical attempt to change the world. Because it is a response that facilitates change, emotion is seen by some to be the survival response—the one that enables the individual to adapt to new and threatening situations.

From still another point of view affect is viewed as the expression of psychic energy. It is to the human organism what the consumption of fuel or power is to a mechanical system. Whitehead writes that "The key notion from which such a construction should start is that the energetic activity considered in physics is the emotional intensity entertained in life." Just as the physicist recognizes the relation between energy and heat, so the common language speaks of the heat of emotion. The energy that is experienced as emotion is variously described as psychonic energy, bio energy, nervous energy, vital energy. An affect is experienced when there is an alteration in the level of this energy. Understood as energy, it is easy to see how affect relates to survival and the facilitation of change.

Connections with the Unconscious, with Value and Meaning

The concept of emotion as energy leads naturally to the idea of affect as an expression of the unconscious. If emotional changes are watched carefully, it is apparent that many of them come from somewhere besides one's consciously held ideas or values. For a moment imagine a law-abiding person driving down the freeway carefully, competently, and completely unaware of an authority problem. Suddenly he hears a siren and glances in his rearview mirror to see flashing red lights. His heart begins to pound, and his blood pressure jumps; his body, which seldom lies about such things, tells him he is more afraid of policemen than he had any idea. What Jerome Frank has called the assumptive world, lying hidden underneath the consciously known attitudes, has triggered an emotional reaction. Each of us, down under, finds a world pictured by such assumptions—about men in uniform, chocolate ice cream, long hair, hospitals and doctors, females, a house like the one we grew up in . . . you name it.

Thus it has appeared reasonable to formulate the hypothesis of an unconscious reservoir of feelings, attitudes, images, and ideas which have the power to release affect, and at the same time can be known in dreams. Simply establishing this connection opened so much understanding that some psychologists have come close to equating emotion with the unconscious. Psychotherapy starting with Freud has endeavored to discover the unconscious roots of troublesome emotions so that the patient can deal with them. And there is plenty of evidence about changes in people's affective life through trying to understand the dynamics of their unconscious processes. If students do in fact have such assumptive or unconscious worlds so closely linked to affect, then the wise teacher will want to relate to their affectivity as one of the most important ways to facilitate learning.

There is also a close relationship between emotion and significance or value. It is interesting that value judgments are nearly as suspect as affects in many scientific quarters. Yet, as Whitehead has reminded us, emotion as value-experience is actually prior to discrimination in matters of fact. The basic expression of emotion is: Have a care; here is something that matters! In Whitehead's words:

> Importance reveals itself as transitions of emotion. My importance is my emotional worth now . . . something that mat-

ters, by reason of its own self-enjoyment, which includes enjoyment of others and transitions towards the future.

Emotion is the human response when something either threatens the values one knows, or offers great value in itself. Emotion as positive affect, the loving-caring emotion, can draw us towards what is valuable; or, at the opposite pole, as hostility or anger, it can drive us either to run away or annihilate that which repels. At the same time, emotion is one of the ways in which we express our values to others, and so gain understanding of those values and where they may be changing.

Indeed it is difficult to imagine values without affect, and so it is difficult to imagine teaching values without understanding affect or providing the proper emotional climate. One of the characteristics which distinguishes the schizophrenic is his very inability to express appropriate affect. Psychological maturity consists in part in having adequate and appropriate affectivity, and this can hardly be learned apart from personal relationship in an affective situation.

This, in turn, requires the use of images and imagination. The importance of images for the process of putting emotion to work for us—rather than spending the energy it gives fighting it—can hardly be stressed too much. Conceptual ideas rarely stir much emotion, while images, pictures, stories, music, odors, any of them can quickly bring an affective response. Aquinas recognized the importance of this when he said:

> In the present life human contemplation cannot function without images... (and) The image is the principle of our knowledge. It is that from which our intellectual activity begins...

It is believed by many thinkers that the images in dreams are related to emotions, and that this is one way to deal with upsetting emotions since dream images tend to make us aware of them when an emotion is hindered. One of Jung's main points is that a mood or vague, distressing emotion can seldom be dealt with creatively until it is allowed to express itself in images. Freud, in discussing the nature of free-floating anxiety, indicated that there is something to pin down; he wrote in *A General Introduction to Psychoanalysis:*

> With certain affects one seems to be able to see deeper, and to recognize that the core of it, binding the whole complex structure together, is of the nature of a *repetition* of some particular very significant previous experience. This experience could only have been an exceedingly early impression of a universal type, to be found in the previous history of the species rather than of the individual.

With the powerful images of myth, folklore, and drama available, the teacher has in his hands the tools that can touch the emotions of others. The need for concrete representation of affect in the teaching of religion is almost too obvious to mention. In the exercises of Ignatius Loyola we find one example of a discipline using images for spiritual goals. Yet most of religious instruction today has become purely conceptual.

There are those who see artistic expression as a mere sublimation of meaningless energy and emotion. But there are many other thinkers, from the philosophers of ancient Greece to modern times, who consider that affect gives birth to creativity. Aristotle, for instance, carefully showed the relation of classical Greek tragedy to a purging of the emotions. Wordsworth felt that poetry originates from a spontaneous overflow of powerful feelings which are then recollected in tranquillity. Henri Bergson went even further by suggesting that some new emotion, something other than a product of intellect, is the source of every great creation of civilization. To these men and to many others, affect contains the seed of the highest creative expressions of human beings. Emotions, they find, can give rise to imaginative expressions which are the real foundation for human growth and development.

From this point of view emotion is to be sought because it leads to self-actualization and human creativity. If religion is understood as necessarily related to creativity and self-actualization, then there is good reason for us to encourage affectivity as a source of creative power. Whether affect is creative or destructive depends in large part upon the strength of the ego which has to deal with emotion. The teacher's role at this point is the most important one of providing support and guidance, for a fractured ego is seldom creative any longer.

When man is understood as having access to an objective spiritual world, as well as to only a physical one, affect can be seen as an aspect of human life which gives access to the other spiritual dimension. William James touches upon this matter in *The Varieties of Religious Experience:*

> ... Just so are the passions themselves gifts,—gifts to us, from sources sometimes low and sometimes high; but almost always nonlogical and beyond our control... Gifts, either of the flesh or of the spirit; and the spirit bloweth where it listeth; and the world's materials lend their surface passively to all gifts alike....

Jung reminds us that the primitive mind experiences autonomous affect as spirits and suggests that the primitive mind may not be entirely off base in its understanding. The fathers of the Christian church wrote again and again about the ways in which affects are known, expressing clearly that these are the media through which man reaches out to the world of the spirit. As Hillman has suggested in summarizing this view, it is only through emotion that we are led to higher spiritual and aesthetic awareness, and to God. Should this be correct, religious education is certainly closely linked to affectivity.

Conclusions for the Teaching of Religion

One thing at least is clear. Affectivity is a complex subject that quite naturally stirs almost as many opinions as there are people thinking about it. But there also appears to be a pattern in the variety of ideas we have reviewed. It seems, in fact, that how a man understands and values emotion depends primarily on his basic philosophic stance, his view of the universe. So long as the world is viewed as a closed and rationally understandable, mechanical system, with the human being just one of the many parts of that system, then affect is seen as valueless. It can only be disruptive, disordering. When people realize, however, that their knowledge of themselves and their world is not quite so complete, then emotion becomes an avenue of discovery, and provides the energy for seeking. When the world is imagined as many-dimensional, with unexpected contents and organizations, then new dimensions and new quests keep opening up before us. We can no longer see ourselves as perfectly organized and determined. It is our affects that open new realms and set us upon new quests. Of course there is risk in dealing directly with affect; it can overwhelm the ego. But is life without risk really life at all?

The recent objective studies of the importance of affectivity in education give some indication that purely rational learning itself may be more of an ideal than a reality. These studies have also shown that education which seeks to bring changes of behavior, as well as of intellectual ideas, requires some use of affectivity. Our survey of theories of affect gives good ground for expecting that this would be the case.

Cognitive knowledge of concepts and ideas does not necessarily result in action, as James Michael Lee and others have demonstrated quite clearly in *Toward a Future for Religious Education*. Therefore, the competent teacher who wishes to open up new ways of behavior to the student through religious classes will use the emotional climate as one tool. And since emotion can be taught only through emotion, the teacher's own emotional development, awareness, and maturity will have a profound effect upon that climate, as well as influencing the kind of learning that takes place in the religion class. Because affect has ramifications for people's lives in all aspects of living, it is important that students, either adults or children, learn how to deal with their affects in the most constructive and creative ways. Further, since affect is closely linked to value, those who are interested in teaching values will wish to understand affect and its relation to values. And since there is also a strong possibility of close relationship between emotion and spirit, education in dealing with affect will be a part of education towards and in the Spirit.

Certainly there are many implications for the teaching of reli-

gion. Whatever else we may say about affect—flattering or
otherwise—it is an agent of change. In our present world situation, when a materialistic world view has all but engulfed the
Western world, it will probably be necessary to help students
learn to use their emotions in order to break out of an all too
confining world view. Genuine belief in spirit, as expressed in
behavior, is a rarity in our modern world. It is doubtful whether
a change of the magnitude required to know and deal with this
spiritual dimension can be brought about other than through
affect.

Affect is most clearly related to values and conduct. If teachers
want to have religious ideas translated from cognitive knowledge
into behavioral action, they will use class situations to facilitate
the controlled expression of affect. Opportunities will be given
for movement, artistic expression, creativity, openness, process.
Effective learning seldom takes place except under these conditions. While there is need for more adequate discussion of the
nature of the most creative affects, it is easy to see that experiences of care and loving concern will most readily help individuals find their own depth of affect, and how to express it in relation to others. If the Christian idea that God is love is correct,
we can hardly understand or deal with God on a purely intellectual basis, as Jung points out so clearly in the closing pages
of *Memories, Dreams, Reflections*. It is difficult to teach love
except through love, and this is affect. Even then, a measure of
anxiety is involved.

Teachers of religion will encourage the use of imagery, pictures, symbols, myths, and stories, all of which reach to the
affective depth of the individual and influence his behavior. One
reason that Christianity has been so effective through the ages is
its use of rites and rituals which have carried meaning far beyond
rational ideas. The eucharist itself is one of the most effective
instruments of learning because it embodies symbols and images
that reach to the affects and so to values and to the Spirit.

Individual teachers can seldom deal with such affective situations wisely unless they can come to a mature and differentiated
emotional life themselves. This involves a deep knowledge of

one's self and one's assumptive world with its charged images and feelings—a knowledge which can hardly be found except within the climate of an accepting community. In addition to knowledge, one needs the wisdom which comes from dealing with one's own affective depth. Without such knowledge and maturity, the affective situation is a dangerous one, for one then has little preparation for what may explode from one's self or another. Luck, rather than mature ease, then determines whether one can react to keep the situation in hand or not.

Our conclusion is a simple one. Its implementation is not so simple. Effective and creative teaching of religion comes at a real cost to the teacher, but the dividends also belong to such a teacher as well as to the students—they come in the form of the deep understanding which results from a mature and wise use of affectivity.

We turn now to ask what reasons Christian theology can possibly give us to expect results from our efforts like those that have been suggested. Is there a Christian view of the world which allows for such possibilities, a view that intelligent and honest people can maintain?

7

A World View for Educating Christians

Theology is the discipline which attempts to bring our knowledge and experience of God into relationship with the rest of our knowledge. This is a big undertaking and a difficult one. It is particularly difficult in a world which keeps adding to the stockpile of knowledge as fast as ours is doing. Theology tries to answer the question: What is the ultimate nature of our world? It must look at a world in which we have such diverse experiences as observing the holocaust of a Hiroshima, seeing scientists manipulate the "fingers" of a robot on Mars, learning of new galaxies and nuclear particles; a world where there are neuroses, psychoses, and black ghettos like Watts; a world also of dreams and extrasensory perception, and even of religious experiences. Christian theology ought to relate all these experiences and realities to the life and teaching of Jesus of Nazareth, to the New Testament.

A great amount of popular theology rejects—either implicitly or explicitly—about half of the New Testament narrative, not on textual but on theological grounds; the parts rejected, it is said, do not fit into our world view. One reason the church fathers are no longer taken very seriously is that they shared and continued the world view of the New Testament—hence their relevance to the world of today is questioned. This popular theology does not make room for the kind of possibilities for Christian education that we have discussed. If we are to move beyond this present view, our first step is to understand it well enough to see why a change is indicated.

The Existentialists' Influence

Rudolf Bultmann is the clearest, most consistent and most daringly frank of the theologians who voice this rejection while still maintaining a Christian stance. In his *Kerygma and Myth* he states with disarming frankness and clarity that Christians must accept the world view in which they find themselves, and that there is nothing they can do to change it. The theologian, he insists, must interpret the Christian message in terms of that world view. The view which Bultmann believes is authoritative is that of the existentialism of Martin Heidegger—a monism which holds that man can know only his own conscious existence, which can be understood through ontological analysis, and that we have no experience of any transpersonal realm or of any reality other than the personal.

Bultmann suggests that we demythologize the New Testament to make it conform to this world view. This means rejecting all the stories of healing; of angels, demons, and the devil (along with heaven and hell); of tongues and prophecy and instances of precognition or other extrasensory perception. It means rejection of all the dreams and visions that were recorded in both the Old and the New Testaments showing how God most often revealed himself to individuals. (A friend and I carefully read the New Testament to spot those verses which refer to such experiences or which derive their meaning from reference to them. We discovered that 49 per cent—3,874 verses out of the total of 7,957—are thus "infected," and that many contain references to more than one of the elements in question.)

The kind of rejection that is suggested puts the sincere Christian in an awkward position. Yet this is the tack liberal Christianity has been on for decades. Even Barthian theology rejects the same five elements of "myth" as operative in human experience today. Barth holds that one is supposed to accept these elements in the New Testament itself by the jump of faith, in a sophisticated dispensationalism.

Unless one has some understanding of the existentialism of Heidegger and the phenomenology of Husserl, it is simply impossible to comprehend intelligently the thinking of Bultmann,

Barth, Bonhoeffer, or their popularizer John A. T. Robinson and the logical fruition of their ideas in the "God is dead" movement. Accepting their theological ideas without this basic philosophic understanding is like taking part in a drag race blindfolded. Both Bultmann and Barth had close personal friendships with Heidegger and Husserl. Both were deeply influenced, if not overawed, by these academic philosophers who successively held the chair of philosophy at Freiberg, and whose thinking formed the basis for existentialism.

Rejection of the Nonmaterial

There is certainly nothing final about the philosophical formulations of Husserl, Heidegger, and the other existentialists. There are other expressions of modern thinking fully as significant, and some of them exert even more pervasive influence. Beyond the fact that it leads into rejection of half of the New Testament narrative as "myth," undercutting all Christian theology up to Aquinas, this philosophical point of view has some very serious flaws.

In the first place, recent existentialism accepts without question the basic theory of knowledge advanced by Aristotle as refined through Descartes—the theory that man has experience only through the senses and consequently only with material reality. Existentialism therefore assumes the monistic position that there is no reality other than consciously received experience. This is a strange development of Hegelian idealism. The basic dualistic theory of knowledge of Plato, Jesus, and the church fathers is rejected without even the barest consideration.

Existentialism then tries to escape from a confining naturalism by deriving knowledge of essences and transcendent reality through what is called ontological analysis, which is essentially deductive thinking under a new name. The whole point of view is quite unintelligible to the scientific mind, which has learned so much through inductive thinking and which has found that knowledge is expanded and deepened as new facts are presented that make old hypotheses inadequate. For instance, the old atomic theory had to be changed completely to take into account the one extremely rare natural phenomenon of radioactivity. The reflective scientist believes that both knowledge and the knower are real, and that one's knowledge of both increases in depth with new data. The philosophy of science which has formulated the successful scientific methods of today into a system of thought has produced some mature thinking quite at variance with that of existentialism.

Indeed, it is noteworthy how few members of the scientific community are touched by existentialism. Today's scientists are much closer to the thinking of Carl Jung of Zurich, who in his psychological studies laid a base for an understanding of Christian experience. Once the data of religious experience relating to nonphysical reality are thus admitted into an inductive system, an adequate basis for Christian theology is present.

The Unconscious Overlooked

The other serious flaw in existentialism is its failure to consider the unconscious. Just before his untimely death in 1962, Maurice Merleau-Ponty, the most recent and in some ways the most important existential thinker, pointed out that Husserl had looked at the concept of the unconscious mind and, finding it logically inconsistent, never again considered the findings of depth psychology. This particular gap in Husserl's thinking was passed on to the other existentialists, none of whom ever took into consideration the findings of Freud, Jung, and their followers. Thus depth psychology and the unconscious are ignored by Heidegger, Jaspers, Marcel, and Sartre, and also by the theologians Bultmann, Bonhoeffer, Robinson, and van Buren. While these men do consider dread and anxiety, they ignore the works of people who have spent their lives dealing with the problem. The whole development of depth psychology had been skipped over by these philosophers until Merleau-Ponty turned his attention to it.

Similar criticism could be leveled at F. R. Tennant, John Baillie, and Douglas MacIntosh, who have written on the subject of religious knowledge from the point of view of rationalistic theology. For the most part it could also be applied to the "God is dead" theology, which carries the thinking of rational theology and existentialism to a logical conclusion.

Yet the concept of the unconscious is not completely new to philosophy. As we have seen, it began to develop very soon after Descartes had clearly defined the idea of consciousness. In the process of developing a method of investigating experience based on analytical geometry, Descartes arrived at the idea that man should restrict his investigation to that which is clearly rational and conscious. The recent theologians do not seem to notice that this idea was inspired by a dream experience which not only brought Descartes himself "from chaos to clarity" but also started the modern scientific method. By the nineteenth century many philosophic discussions were being devoted to the unconscious; among them those of Carus and von Hartmann were the most important. Henri Bergson, in a little book written before he knew of Freud, suggested that learning about the unconscious would become the most important undertaking of the twentieth century.

Freud, however, was the first to show that the dream provided an empirical tool for understanding and dealing with the contents of the unconscious. He saw in the unconscious the most diverse psychic contents, ranging from yesterday's memories to archaic racial experiences. His book, *The Interpretation of Dreams,* provided one of the foundations for modern thinking.

Jung simplified Freud's theory of dream interpretation and showed how dreams involve essentially symbolic rather than rational or conceptual thinking. He also provided empirical evidence that man has direct contact not only with primitive and archaic contents of the collective unconscious, but also with contents beyond human consciousness. And in some of his final writings Freud came close to a similar point of view.

It is obvious that in this matter Jung's thought approaches that of the New Testament and the patristic tradition, yet his conclusions stemmed from his medical practice, not from any esoteric religious ideas or far-fetched misunderstandings. In fact, he found some of the elements in the New Testament which Bultmann considers the most scandalously "mythological" to be among the most revealing and significant experiences of the people who came to him for treatment. He supported his point of view not with logic or reason alone but with the empirical evidence of his patients' actual experience and by a careful study of his own inner experience. He described these experiences in meticulous detail in the nineteen volumes of his collected works.

Plato and the Church Fathers

Jung was philosophically the most sophisticated of the modern psychologists. He knew modern philosophy well, and he was well trained. Because he used the methods described by the philosophy of science, his data were subjected to a rigorous scientific empiricism. Because he knew that in his last book he was stepping down from a strictly scientific empiricism, by his own wish his autobiography was not included in his collected works. Because the facts demanded rejection of the materialism and rationalism in which he was raised, Jung's mature thinking resembles that of Plato and the church fathers, as well as that of Kant, Carus, von Hartmann, Bergson, and Lovejoy.

In his theory of knowledge Plato differed basically from Aristotle, who held that man has no knowledge of nonphysical reality other than that gained through rational analysis. Aristotle insisted that while man can know the forms resident in matter through sense experience and reason, there is no nonphysical reality known through experience.

Plato, on the other hand, believed that in addition to sense experience and reason human beings also have direct knowledge of a nonphysical realm of reality which exists independently of material reality, and that in this realm their "ideas" are an important content. They gain access to this reality not through reason but through what Plato described as "divine madness." This possession of consciousness by something different from the conscious mind, by the divine, is experienced in prophecy, in healing, in artistic inspiration, and in love—all of which are found at times in the dream experience. These experiences have the same autonomy as experiences of the physical world. In depth psychology these four that Plato described would be termed knowledge coming through the unconscious.

Christian theology was born when Justin Martyr discovered the harmony between the thought of Plato, the experiences of the early church and that church's story of Jesus. It came to fruition as Origen, Athanasius, the great Cappadocians, and Augustine developed their thought from essentially the same insight. Its rebirth, out of that insight, might occur today if Christian thinkers come to realize that the experiences of Jesus and the early church are in harmony not only with Plato but with the most advanced modern thinking, with the thinking of students of depth psychology, particularly that of Jung. This could have happened in the seventeenth century if the church of that time had been open enough to consider the thinking of the Cambridge Platonists, of Ralph Cudworth, John Norris, and the Earl of Shaftesbury. As L. L. Whyte suggests in *The Unconscious Before Freud,* "a Christian post-Cudworth school of scientific thought might have enjoyed the world prestige of Marx and Freud together, and more. But [the Christian churches] preferred the status quo."

Jung's scientific understanding, which offers a similar opportunity today, was expressed very clearly in one letter to me. In it Jung set forth his belief that man has contact with two phenomenal worlds, two experiences which can be known: the objective physical reality which comes through to us in sense experience, and the equally objective psychic or nonphysical world which is known through experiences of the unconscious. It is this latter reality which is spoken of in so many ways in Paul's letters and the gospels and which was called the spiritual world by the church fathers. This epistemology is supported with great philosophic acumen by A. O. Lovejoy. In *The Revolt Against Dualism,* one of the most careful studies of how we know, Lovejoy continues the tradition of Plato and of Augustine, a tradition that was also expressed by Kant, C. G. Carus, and von Hartmann.

The New Testament as Handbook

According to Jung and others who have emulated his approach, nowhere is a better understanding of this entire nonphysical reality, both good and evil, displayed than in the life and teachings of Jesus. Some of these people have suggested that the New Testament is the best handbook we have on psychological integration and maturity. Christianity genuinely practiced not only resolves many neuroses but leads toward both psychological and religious wholeness. In his autobiography, where he took a broader look than his strictly scientific approach usually permitted, Jung clearly equated the collective aspects of the unconscious—which he had continued to describe in practical terms throughout his works—with the spiritual realm described by the church. In this view, it is the task of the physical scientist to deal with physical phenomena, to learn more about them in depth, whereas it is the task of psychology and religion to understand and deal with the psychic world, the world of spirit.

Because of these conclusions Jung went along with most students of mythology today in seeing myth as something very different from the idea of mere prescientific cosmology, an idea which is one key to the thinking of Bultmann. Instead, modern students see myth as people's attempt to convey in images those experiences which come to them from the autonomous nonphysical world. Because these experiences do not come from the physical world but consist of everything from yesterday's subliminal impressions and forgotten reactions to nonpersonal psychic elements, they require the imaginative form of myth.

The dream is the individual's personal myth, expressing one's daily interaction with this nonphysical world. Until Aquinas' attempt to baptize Aristotle into Christianity the church almost uniformly accepted the understanding of the church fathers that God spoke directly to man, most often in dreams and visions— the way par excellence by which divine revelation came. It is sobering to remember that in the ancient church only the Arians were followers of Aristotle, to whom the dream represented something which does not exist.

Jung has been one of the most successful practicing psychia-trists in the brief history of that profession; even so, he may well be more important philosophically and religiously than psychologically. His works, based on fifty years of work with patients from every corner of the world, many of whom recov-ered, provide a theory of knowledge and a philosophic point of view which takes in the full gamut of human experience and upon which a surprisingly orthodox Christianity can be based. In this light the contents of the New Testament need not be de-mythologized; rather, their mythological elements can be un-derstood as intrusions by the objective nonphysical world into the physical one. Even the teaching of Jesus about the kingdom of God begins to have new relevance when understood in this way. When one sees the kind of experiences described in the New Testament repeated in the life of someone close to him, or in the psychiatrist's office, one is no longer skeptical of the New Testament or of early church tradition.

A Christianity with this kind of understanding and experience is competent to deal not only with people's ideas but with their deep inner conflicts, their neuroses, their lostness, their proj-ections onto the blacks, even their determination to go to war. This kind of Christianity is as intellectually defensible as the watered-down variety. And it can bring the individual to the kind of transforming experience which was so common in the first five centuries of the church's life and is still familiar to those we speak of as saints. How much the world needs such a Chris-tianity at the present time! The task of theology is not so much to interpret Christianity in terms harmonious with the latest world view, but rather to find and formulate a workable world view which will again bring the reality of Christian experience into the picture.

Within the world view of the New Testament, as Jung and others open it up for us, education in Christian understanding and experience is possible. The goal of this education is to create the conditions wherein individuals, in all of their complexity, may develop to their maximum potential, embodying as much of the Spirit of God as possible. The early church fathers held that Christ became what we are in order that we might become what he is. The task of Christian education is to create the conditions so that this may happen, so that through the communication of Christian understanding and experience men may come to know God.

There is no more important task in our modern world, and no other agency but the church and its members exists to do it.

References

The quotations found in each chapter are cited in the order of their appearance:

CHAPTER 3

Death to Life, Chicago, ARGUS Communications, 1968, pp. 34 and 37. Karl Jasper provides one article in this anthology.

C. G. Jung, *Memories, Dreams, Reflections*. Recorded and edited by Aniela Jaffé. New York, Pantheon Books, 1963, pp. 353 f.

A.-J. Festugière, (in the *Revue de Théologie et de Philosophie*, 1961, p. 31), quoted by E. R. Dodds, *Pagan and Christian in an Age of Anxiety*. Cambridge (Eng.), The University Press, 1965, p. 138.

Laurens van der Post, *The Face Beside the Fire*. New York, William Morrow & Company, Inc., 1953, pp. 10, 79, and 268.

Rudolf Steiner, *Knowledge of the Higher Worlds and Its Attainment*. New York, AnthropoSophic Press (1947), p. 40.

St. Ambrose, *Duties of the Clergy*, Book II, Chapter VII, sec. 37, 36

Louis Evely, *That Man Is You*. Westminster, Maryland, The Newman Press, 1966, pp. 16 and 26.

Laurens van der Post, *op. cit.*, p. 112.

CHAPTER 4

A.-J. Festugière, quoted by E. R. Dodds, *loc cit.*

CHAPTER 6

Fellings and Emotions: The Wittenberg Symposium. Edited by Martin L. Reymert. Worcester, Massachusetts, Clark University Press, 1928: D. T. Howard, "A Functional Theory of the Emotions," p. 147.

Ibid.: Harvey A. Carr, "The Differentia of an Emotion," p. 231.

James Hillman, *Emotion: A Comprehensive Phenomenology of Theories and Their Meanings for Therapy*. Evanston, Illinois, Northwestern University Press, 1964, p. 190. I am indebted to Hillman for his excellent study from which much of this material is drawn.

Fellings and Emotions, op. cit.: Knight Dunlap, "Emotion as a Dynamic Background," p. 151.

Ronald T. Hyman, Ed., *Teaching: Vantage Points for Study.* Philadelphia, J. B. Lippincott Company, 1968: William H. Stavsky, "Using the Insights of Psychotherapy in Teaching," p. 175. This book contains a number of excellent articles by various students working on the relation of emotion to learning.

Alfred North Whitehead, *Modes of Thought.* Cambridge (Eng.), The University Press, 1938, pp. 231 f.

Ibid. pp. 160 f.

Thomas Aquinas, *Summa Theologiæ*, II, II, 180. 5 ad 2; and *In Librum Boethii de Trinitate*, VI.2 ad 5.

Sigmund Freud, *A General Introduction to Psychoanalysis.* New York, Washington Square Press, Inc., 1960, p. 403.

William James, *The Varieties of Religious Experience.* New York, Longmans, Green, and Co., 1920, p. 151.

CHAPTER 7

Lancelot Law Whyte, *The Unconscious before Freud.* New York, Basic Books, Inc., 1960, p. 96.

Bibliography

Henri Bergson, *The Two Sources of Morality and Religion.* New York, Henry Holt and Company, 1935.

Rudolf Bultmann, *Kerygma and Myth: A Theological Debate.* Edited by Hans-Werner Bartsch. London, S.P.C.K., 1957.

Harold William Burgess, *An Invitation to Religious Education.* Mishawaka, Indiana, Religious Education Press Inc., 1975.

Carl G. Carus, *Psyche, on the Development of the Soul.* Part 1. Edited by James Hillman. New York, Spring Publications, 1970.

Kenneth E. Eble, *A Perfect Education.* New York, Collier Books, 1968.

Jerome D. Frank, M.D., *Persuasion and Healing: A Comparative Study of Psychotherapy.* 1st edition. New York, Schocken Books, 1969.

Ronald Goldman, *Readiness for Religion.* New York, Seabury Press, Inc., 1968.

———, *Religious Thinking from Childhood to Adolescence.* New York, Humanities Press, 1964.

M. Esther Harding, *The Way of All Women.* New York, Harper & Row, 1975.

James Hillman, *Insearch: Psychology and Religion.* New York, Charles Scribner's Sons, 1968.

Kenneth G. Johnson, *General Semantics: An Outline Survey.* Madison, Extension Division, University of Wisconsin, 1960.

C. G. Jung, *Collected Works.* Princeton, New Jersey, Princeton University Press:

Vol. 6, *Psychological Types,* 1971.

Vol. 11, *Psychology and Religion: West and East.* 1970.

Vol. 12, *Psychology and Alchemy.* 1968.

Vol. 17, *The Development of Personality.* 1954.

———, *Modern Man in Search of a Soul.* New York, Harcourt Brace Jovanovich, Inc., 1955.

———, *Two Essays on Analytical Psychology.* Princeton, New Jersey, Princeton University Press, 1972.

Carl G. Jung and others, *Man and his Symbols.* New York, Dell Publishing Co., Inc., 1964.

Morton T. Kelsey, "Confronting Inner Violence." *The Journal of Pastoral Counseling* 8, No. 1 (Spring-Summer 1973): 11–22.

———, *Encounter with God.* Also, *Study Guide.* Minneapolis, Bethany Fellowship, Inc., 1975.

———, "Facing Death and Suffering: A Group Experiment in Affective Learning." *Lumen Vitae* 28 (1973), No. 2: 281–95.

———, *God, Dreams, and Revelation.* Minneapolis, Augsburg Publishing House, 1974.

———, *Healing and Christianity.* New York, Harper & Row, 1973.

———, *Myth, History and Faith.* New York, Paulist Press, 1974.

———, *The Other Side of Silence: A Guide to Christian Meditation.* New York, Paulist Press, 1976.

Fritz Kunkel, *Creation Continues.* Waco, Texas, Word Books, 1973.

James Michael Lee, *The Flow of Religious Instruction: A Social-Science Approach.* Mishawaka, Indiana, Religious Education Press Inc., 1975.

———, *The Shape of Religious Instruction: A Social-Science Approach.* Mishawaka, Indiana, Religious Education Press Inc., 1975.

Eve Lewis, *Children and Their Religion.* New York, Sheed and Ward, Inc., 1962.

Arthur O. Lovejoy, *The Revolt Against Dualism.* New York, W. W. Norton & Company, Inc., 1930.

Maria F. Mahoney, *The Meaning in Dreams and Dreaming.* New York, The Citadel Press, 1970.

Isabel Briggs Myers, *Introduction to Type.* Privately printed (321 Dickinson Avenue, Swarthmore, Pennsylvania 19081), 1970.

———, *Manual: The Myers-Briggs Type Indicator.* Princeton, New Jersey, Educational Testing Service, 1963.

Howard Ozmon, *Dialogue in the Philosophy of Education.* Columbus, Ohio, Charles E. Merrill Publishing Company, 1972.

Hugh V. Perkins, *Human Development and Learning.* 2nd edition. Belmont, California, Wadsworth Publishing Co., 1974.

Josef Pieper, *Enthusiasm and Divine Madness.* New York, Harcourt Brace and World, 1964.

Carl R. Rogers, *Freedom to Learn.* Columbus, Ohio, Charles E. Merrill Publishing Company, 1969.

John A. Sanford, *Dreams: God's Forgotten Language.* Philadelphia, J. B. Lippincott Company, 1968.

———, *The Kingdom Within: A Study of the Inner Meaning of Jesus' Savings.* Philadelphia, J. B. Lippincott Company, 1970.

Merton P. Strommen, Ed., *Research on Religious Development: A Comprehensive Handbook.* New York, Hawthorn Books, Inc., 1971.

Paul Tillich, *Theology of Culture.* New York, Oxford University Press, 1959.

Marie-Louise von Franz and James Hillman, *Lectures on Jung's Typology*. New York, Spring Publications, 1971.

Frances Wickes, *The Inner World of Childhood*. New York, Appleton-Century, 1966.

Acknowledgments

The editor wishes to express his thanks for permission to use articles by Morton Kelsey which originally appeared in slightly different form in the following publications:
1. "Can Christians Be Taught?," *Your Church,* XXI (March–April, 1975), pp. 9–41.
2. "Praying in Images," unpublished manuscript.
3. "The Art of Christian Love," Dove Publications, 1974, 44 pp.
4. "Communicating Religion," permission from *Encounter with God* by Morton Kelsey, published and copyright 1972, Bethany Fellowship, Inc. Minneapolis, Minnesota.
5. "God, Education and the Unconscious," *Religious Education,* LXV (May–June, 1970), pp. 227–234—by permission of the Religious Education Association, 409 Prospect St., New Haven, CT 06510. Membership subscription available for $20.00 per year.
6. "The Place of Affect in Religious Education: Psychodynamics of Affectivity and Emotion," *Lumen Vitae,* XXVI (March 1971), pp. 68–80.
7. "Is the World View of Jesus Outmoded?," *The Christian Century,* LXXXVI (January 22, 1969), pp. 112–115. By permission from Christian Century Foundation.

Further thanks is expressed for permission to use extended quotations from the following publications:
1. Louis Evely, *That Man Is You.* Westminster, Maryland, The Newman Press, 1966.
2. C. G. Jung, *Memories, Dreams, Reflections.* Recorded and edited by Aniela Jaffé. New York, Pantheon Books, 1963.
3. Laurens van der Post, *The Face Beside the Fire.* New York, William Morrow & Company, Inc., 1953.